SIMON DEWHU

SECRETS OF BETTER SKIING

by

SIMON DEWHURST

SECRETS OF BETTER SKIING

SIMON DEWHURST

Simon Dewhurst has been a ski teacher for forty five years. He has taught in Norway, Switzerland, Italy, France and North America. He has run ski chalets in the French Alps, skied 108mph as an FIS speed skier, and made several films. He lives in the UK near Liverpool where he writes.

Secrets of Better Skiing was first published in 2006 on the internet and has been edited many times since then. This is the first print edition.

SECRETS OF BETTER SKIING

ISBN-13: 978-1542595179
ISBN-10: 1542595177

Text copyright © 2017 Simon Dewhurst All Rights Reserved
Cover design and photograph © Simon Dewhurst 2017

SIMON DEWHURST

TABLE OF CONTENTS

INTRODUCTION	9
1A – BASIC CONSIDERATIONS	14
EQUIPMENT - THE SKI	14
REVERSE CAMBER ETC.	16
RELEASE BINDINGS	18
BOOTS	20
POLES	21
FITNESS	22
1B – BASIC CONSIDERATIONS	24
STYLE & BALANCE	24
FALLING	27
BODY POSITIONS	28
ANGULATION	30
ANTICIPATION	30
POLE PLANT	31
EDGING AND CARVING	32
SELF ASSESSMENT	33
2 – REVERSION TECHNIQUE	36
THE START	37
THE SNOWPLOUGH (Stem or Wedge)	37
THE SNOWPLOUGH TURN	37

THE STEM TURN	39
THE STEM CHRISTIE	40
THE CHRISTIE OR PARALLEL TURN	42
3 – SOME THEORY & EXERCISES	44
HOW DO YOU TURN A SKI?	46
UNWEIGHTING 1 'DOWN SLOW & UP QUICK'	46
UNWEIGHTING 2 'DOWN QUICK & UP QUICK'	47
UNWEIGHTING 3 BUMPS	47
STEERING	48
4 – PRACTICAL WORK	49
LEARNING POSITIONS	49
EDGING EXERCISES	49
A LONG CONTROLLED TURN	52
SHORT (SWING) TURNS - STANDARD	55
5 – SKIING IN THE BUMPS	59
FIRST EXERCISES	60
LINKING TURNS TOGETHER	61
KNEE EXERCISE	63
GETTING THE RHYTHM	64
6 – OFF PISTE	66
POWDER SKIING TECHNIQUE	66
SKI THE STEEP - JUMP TURNS	70
OFF PISTE IN THE SPRING	74
SKI THE STEEP IN POWDER	76
7 – ADVANCED TURNS	79
LONG FAST TURNS - INTRODUCTION	79

SAFETY AT SPEED	79
THE LAZY FAST TURN	80
THE FAST TURN - EDGING	81
GIANT SLALOM & LATERAL PROJECTION	82
THE POWER TURN	83
CONTRE VIRAGE - TAIL SLIDE	84
SHORT TURN & LATERAL PROJECTION	85
WEDEL TURNS	86
JET TURNS	86
8 – AVALANCHES AND SNOWCRAFT	88
AVALANCHES	95
SNOWCRAFT	93
9A – GOODBYE TO THE BAD STUFF	96
FEAR, FITNESS AND FALLING	96
LOSS OF NERVE	97
LACK OF CONFIDENCE	99
FALLING	100
BAD EQUIPMENT	102
9B – G OODBYE TO THE BAD STUFF	103
SKI SCHOOL	103
PUTTING A BEGINNER ON THE RIGHT TRACK	105
HOLIDAYS, MONEY AND MOTIVATION	106
CORRECTIING FAULTS	107
Upper Body Position	108
Weight Transfer	108
Sitting Back	109

10 – DIVERSIONS	111
SPEED SKIING	111
FREESTYLE - BASIC BALLET PROGRAMME	113
JUMPING	115
The Pre-Jump	115
The Jump - going for Air	116
Cliffs Rocks and Cornices	117
THE UPHILL SKI - Food for Thought	119
11 – SNOW TYPES & HOW TO SKI THEM	123
RED SNOW AT ANY TEMPERATURE	124
ICE	124
SKI MAINTENANCE FOR ICE	125
SNOW – AIR TEMPERATURE ABOVE 0°C	128
Fresh snow	128
Old snow	128
SNOW FROM 0 to -10°C degrees	129
SNOW LOWER THAN -10°C degrees	131
GLOSSARY	132
RULES OF THE SLOPES	141
OFF PISTE RULES	143

SIMON DEWHURST

INTRODUCTION

*Högt upp på fjället finns ingen polis
där kan man stå naken och släppa en fis.*
High up on the mountain you'll find no old bill
You can stand with no clothes on and break wind at will.
Swedish poem - anon

It was a cold night, perhaps minus twenty Celsius, and I was standing outside a cabin in the mountains of central Norway. The snow squeaked underfoot and the hairs up my nose were starting to freeze. In the silence I could hear my heart beating and my breath was clouding in the crystalline air. What a great day, what an amazing thing this skiing game is, heavens above just look at the stars, hell it's cold, am I going round and round or is it the mountains or is it the stars, who knows, who cares, what a great day, what about tomorrow, what about some more aquavit.

Most of us had only been skiing for a week. One had given up, but the rest of us were well and truly hooked. Despite the battering and the bruises, the crashes, the ribald laughter, the snow clogging every orifice, the thumping headaches the next day from aquavit and beer, we still came back to the ski school every morning for more punishment from a gnarled and weather beaten Norwegian farmer called Arne Geilo.

Skiing has been my passion for nearly fifty years. It was this two week holiday back in 1968 that started the rot. Since then I have given up potentially lucrative careers as a dry cleaner delivery man, a city slicker in the unit trust business, a steeplechase jockey, and an actor to name but a few. Every year when the first leaves began to fall from the trees a little voice in the back of my head got louder and louder – it's time to go – it's time for the snow. I didn't argue. It was a soft sell – the thrill of speed, the high from thin mountain air, the friendships born of like minded souls, and the challenge of the hill that never let you forget who was really the master.

I would like to think that you have come across this book for the same reason that still draws me every time I see the word 'skiing' in print – the little frisson of excitement, the feeling that you're in the wrong place, the possibility that by reading about it you're going to be that much closer to the action.

You will only find one set of diagrams in this book. I want you to be transported by your imagination, which of course can take you anywhere you want.

I would like to think that something on these pages will motivate you in this way, and get you even closer to the action of power skiing, controlled skiing, *real* skiing.

***

As a teach yourself book 'Secrets of Better Skiing' is slightly unusual. It starts a short way into the learning process because I do not believe that beginners can be taught *initially* from a book. After much observation it is obvious that there are an enormous number of skiers who seemed to have reached a dead end at quite an early stage of learning, and although keen to improve, are unable to do so. This book is dedicated to them!

Of course there are not really secrets of better skiing technique because a few people know them already. They are only a minority of skiers, however, so for the vast majority of skiers I see and observe, this book *will* appear as a revelation.

Let me give you an example. I often suggest to people that they should try going off trail and experience the delights of skiing on spring snow high up on a glacier with just a few friends, a picnic, and the solitude of the mountains. They usually look at me with a blank expression. Am I a madman to suggest that they should leave the crowded, man made, sometimes bumpy piste for the complete unknown? They invariably reply that they wouldn't know how to ski in those conditions, or that it would be dangerous, or that it would waste a day of their valuable piste bashing time. The fact that the adventure I am suggesting could by no stretch of the imagination live up to their fears has no effect on them.

It's a bit like the McDonalds syndrome. Would we rather try an unknown restaurant in a street of restaurants or the McDonalds slap bang in the middle of them? (I'd like to think that none of you try McDonalds but that's getting off the point) It is the unknown that frightens people and puts them off. Familiarity in this case does not breed contempt, it breeds contentment. We think that we are happier in a familiar situation and are therefore unwilling to try anything new. So this book *does* reveal facts that the vast majority of skiers did not know about before.

If you have reached the standard of skiing where this book starts, and can ski green runs through to red after a fashion, then you *will* be able to go off on adventures like the one I describe without having to improve your technique at all! I have *never* taken people on one of these trips who have been disappointed with the terrain they have skied over and the sights they have seen. There would have been times during such a trip when they forgot their technique completely and skied all the better for it.

There are of course the frustrated skiers out there of a more adventurous nature who would love to improve their technique, but do not really have an idea how to go about it. They really *do* want to ski off piste in powder snow, they really *do* want to master the bumps, they really *would* like to do powerful carved turns, they really *would* like to ski fast, they really *would* like to jump off rocks. Well it's not difficult!

If you read this book and do what it says then you will be able to – I promise! I have made it as simple as I can with the minimum of technical stuff to achieve the maximum effect. I have taken a fairly light hearted approach to the whole business to minimise the bullshit that in places permeates the sport. Skiing is supposed to be fun – it will be even more fun when you have read 'Secrets of Better Skiing'.

I do have one or two apologies to make. First of all I have mixed up miles with kilometers, Celsius with Fahrenheit, feet with metres etc. Marooned on the edge of Europe we have lately become a cultural melting pot that cannot tell its ounces from its grammes. That's my excuse. Secondly I have never pandered to the philosophy of political correctness. If it's fat it's fat, and if like me it's bald – it's bald.

Do read the glossary at the end and refer to it whenever you need to. It is not just an explanation of terms but also a slightly more scientific approach to certain matters.

SIMON DEWHURST

Read through this book once without worrying about the science and technique. Dip into it for a minute or two anywhere you like to memorise a useful snippet. **Read it through a second time, thoroughly**, spending more time on the practical and technical considerations, and it will turn you into an expert! I guarantee it!

1A – BASIC CONSIDERATIONS

EQUIPMENT – THE SKI

To become a better skier, it does help to know a little about the ski, how it works, and how to get the best out of it. It has been around for four thousand years, give or take a year or two, and has come a long way since the one found in a Scandinavian bog five thousand years ago.

It is now a sophisticated machine, and you have probably gathered that the companies making skis are intensely competitive. This means that year on year there is always some interesting technical innovation, and quite often a quantum leap in actual performance. At the time of writing shorter, fatter skis are coming on to the market. There is even a model out there that has winking tip lights. I've no idea where it will end, and I'm not going to discuss in detail the intricacies of a ski's construction – these would fill a book on their own, but it is important to have a basic knowledge of *how* and *why* skis work the way they do.

What kind of skis will you need to improve your skiing? The last few years have seen a great leap forward in ski design. Gone are the recreational skis that had to be as long as your outstretched arm above your head. The optimum length nowadays is anything from 5cm (2in) smaller than you are to 5cm taller than you are as a general rule. So clever is the design that they will grip on ice, go relatively fast, and float through powder. They should be lively and moderately stiff, perhaps 5-10cm taller than you are, and with the bases and edges in excellent condition. The main thing is to try different pairs out and experiment with them.

If you decide to hire or buy from a shop, make sure you go in a quiet time. If you go when the shop is busy, the guy in charge of the skis will look you up and down, and judging by the look on your face, ie: pure terror or cool omniscience, will thrust a pair of skis at you without further ado. Ask the people in the shop for advice. Tell them you are an aggressive skier, and want a pair of performance skis with a bit of welly in them. Hire departments in ski shops have improved dramatically over the years, so you will probably be better off hiring them if you are only skiing for a week or two. If you are lucky enough to be spending a season in the mountains, dig deep, splash out, and buy some – after taking advice you can trust, or trying out a similar pair of course.

How do you know what to get? If you are trying a pair of skis out from the ski shop, or from a friend, take a good look at them first. Look at the bottoms. Are the plastic soles nice and smooth, and free from holes and gouges? The edges should be sharp and smooth with no pit marks in them. They could have been battered by countless previous hirers so test them to see if they have any life left in them. Do this by putting them together, sole to sole, and squeezing them with one hand at the mid point just behind the front binding. There should be a good gap and a certain springiness when you squeeze and let go. Technicians will say there is more to testing a ski in the shop than this, but if there is no gap and no springiness, there ain't much life left in the old thing. To get a better feel you can make some comparisons with some old battered pairs.

The base of the ski needs to be flat without being warped or twisted. Shut one eye and look down the length of the ski to check that it is flat. (Shutting one eye makes you look more professional than keeping both open.) Although the ski remains flat at rest it should have a built in capacity to twist in movement (called torque), but that does not interest us here.

Remember, do talk to the people in the shop and let them know that you that you need an all terrain ski that is going to be worked hard; they will let you try out pairs until you find what suits you, as long as you pay for the hire of course! Remember though that *you will have to work hard to get the best out of good performance skis*, and develop the technique to match, so read on!

REVERSE CAMBER ETC.

Let's just think about how the ski works. It is quite a strange shape really. The pointed bit at the front is turned up and the reason for that is fairly obvious, but why does the ski (viewed horizontally from the side), bend up towards the middle, and why is it wider at the front and the back than in the middle?

There are three words to mull over here, and they are **'camber'**, **'sidecut'**, and **'reverse camber'**. Take a new ski down from the rack in the ski shop and put it flat on the floor. It doesn't have to have a safety binding on it at this stage, and you don't really have to do this in the ski shop if you are shy, so just *imagine* you are doing it. Lay the ski down on the flat floor. The middle is perhaps three quarters of an inch off the ground. Gingerly, push it down with a finger and let it go quickly; it will bounce up. This is the springiness in it - just like you after paying eight weeks in advance for your ski holiday. This upward bend in the ski is known as camber. Now look at the ski from above. It is narrower in the middle than at the tip and the tail. This is known as the sidecut. Now the combination of the camber and the sidecut produces the real goody – the potential for reverse camber. Those of you who know all about this are welcome to skip it. *In my view it is fundamental to better skiing.*

Imagine you are standing still across the fall line on a perfectly smooth steep slope. Your lower ski is in the air because you have lifted your lower leg. Lowering the ski horizontally to the slope, the first parts of the sole to touch the snow will be the tip and the tail. The middle of the ski will not be touching yet because of the camber - the bend upwards. If you lower your leg further and push the middle of the ski further down, *it will only be touching the slope along the whole of its edge after you have bent it past the straight position into the opposite arc or camber.* The distance you can bend it before the whole edge touches depends on the amount of sidecut. The downward arc that the ski now describes is called reverse camber. It is under tension like a spring, not a lot, but more than you did it in the shop because in the shop you had the ski *flat*, and now you have it on its *edge*. If you now start moving forwards down the slope with just the ski on its edge, it will automatically curve over the snow because of the sidecut and the reverse camber. Do you understand this? If you don't then try reading it again until you do. It is a *very important* bit of theory.

We will discuss this later, but it will soon be possible to achieve *added* reverse camber by applying *more* pressure at the right time thereby producing the sort of turn we can only dream about.

Various combinations of stiffness and sidecut determine the type of ski it is. For example, a special slalom ski, designed to do tight turns, will have more sidecut and be stiffer to give more spring than a giant slalom ski designed for longer turns and general recreational skiing. I have not mentioned how length affects the skis' performance - mainly because you probably know already.

If we move away from recreational skiing for a second, the longer the ski the faster it will go. It will also be more difficult to turn, especially at slower speeds. At high speed a longer ski will be much more stable than a short one, and become easier to turn the faster it goes. Having said that, the longest skis of all at 240cm, used for speed skiing, are almost impossible to turn with very little sidecut and no camber - a sixty mile an hour snowplough seems the most effective way to change direction on these monsters. Back to our everyday skiing now, if we are on a recreational performance ski, we can go extremely fast as long as we keep it on its edge, but a lot more of that later.

Summarising all this, the conclusion is that a good pair of skis have the potential to work for *you* as long as you are prepared to put the work into *them*.

RELEASE BINDINGS

These have come a long way since the bone snapping bear traps of the fifties and now we hardly think about them. Anyway, they have become so sophisticated that you need to be a rocket scientist to understand the technicalities.

I must confess that I could always tell you the name of the *ski* I was on, but would be often hard pressed to tell you the name of the binding that was doing such a wonderful job holding me on and letting me go with such *precision*. There are times, however, when they may let you down - usually because they have not been adjusted properly.

There has been a standardised din setting for all makes of binding for many years now so that the numbers on the dials of every make mean the same regardless of the make of binding. They can be adjusted to suit the weight and expertise of a skier - the higher the number the heavier and/or better the skier - *generally*. They should be tightened so that within a reasonable margin they will both hold the skier onto the skis and then let him go when necessary. The back binding releases to prevent him from breaking his leg, and the front one releases to prevent him twisting his knee ligaments. For reasons I won't bother with here, a safe back binding was quite easy to perfect, while a safe front binding was more difficult. This is why there are far fewer broken legs than twisted knee ligaments today. I say that generally bindings should be adjusted to suit the weight of a skier, but his standard and the speed he skis, and the terrain he is skiing on can also be considered.

What I recommend here is that whoever adjusts the skis for you in the shop is aware of your weight and adjusts the bindings accordingly. If they then pre-release and come off when you haven't even made a mistake, check to see whether the back or front one is responsible. If it was the back one it will have opened, and if it was the front one then the back will still be closed. You can usually borrow a screwdriver from the man in the lift hut - don't expect anyone else to do it for you unless you are *very* attractive and they don't mind being sued if you have a bad accident as a result of a maladjusted binding. Tighten in **half clicks** until the binding stops pre-releasing. The harder you ski the higher you will need the settings, **but always crank up in small increments**.

There will sometimes be occasions when the bindings do pre-release in such unusual circumstances that you will know that there is not really a need to do anything about them. Such a thing happened to me about five years ago, when we were skiing in the sun down good hard pack snow. I decided to hang left on to a path out of the sun, and hit it a bit too fast. It was classic ice, hard as rock and bumpy like a ship's bottom and I knew I was in trouble. There was a sharp left turn about fifty yards down but before I was anywhere near it my right ski came off and this was the one I really needed for a left hand turn. I just about got the uphill one to start turning but I couldn't cope with the bumpy ice and hit the lip on the outside of the bend at about thirty miles an hour. Nothing was visible on the other side except the far valley a mile away. At the moment of launch my left ski stopped dead on the upward lip and I flew out of it. I described a perfectly executed parabola about twenty feet above the ground at its highest point with just my boots on, and landed on all fours twenty yards from the bend in soft snow. The people coming up in the gondolas just a few feet away must have really enjoyed themselves.

BOOTS

There are a few things to mention about boots and you probably know about them already. They should be comfortable and hold your heel firmly. If they don't hold your heel firmly you will have to move that much more before the ski does, and you will want them to react *instantaneously* to your every command. Your toes should have a little movement so that the blood continues to circulate. There is nothing more depressing than taking your boots off at the end of the day, not having felt any sensation in your toes since lunch time, and finding that all your toes have turned black. It is sensible therefore to have your own boots as everybody's feet are different; even your own left foot is different from your own right foot. Foam filled customised boots are now the rage so splash out with a load more greenbacks. Go for the most expensive you can afford and they could last a lifetime.

There is still a difference in the stiffness of the boot's outer shell between recreational and competition models. Don't be afraid to go for the highest quality boot you are comfortable with; it will probably feel strange in the shop. Spend a lot of time choosing and clumping around with both boots on. Remember you are going to have to do a lot of walking as well, and not just to the ski lift and back from the bar. By the time you have finished this book you and the mountains will have become one. This means that you may have dispensed with the lift system and will be climbing on foot with a large rucksack and a long beard.

POLES

More seriously, you can actually use any old rubbish when it comes to poles as long as they are the same length, roughly the same light weight, and have some sort of basket. I have always considered trendy looking, expensive poles as a complete waste of money. The way you are going to be skiing shortly means that you will be bending, breaking, and doubtless losing lots of poles. Most shops will probably throw the poles in with whatever you are buying; you will then be able to spend that much more on your boots.

There is, however, *one* important thing to remember about poles. Get some that are slightly shorter than the recommended length for your height. This will improve what is known as your anticipation, and will encourage you to get down lower at the appropriate time. Get them about two inches shorter, and if the assistant in the shop looks at you in a strange fashion, say they are for your little sister, who is two inches smaller than you.

There are several other factors to consider before setting out on the road to Damascus. You may be familiar with some of them, and if you are aware of them all now, the heavy practical stuff will be that much easier to handle later on.

FITNESS

It doesn't involve a great deal of effort for someone who has been skiing for ages to get off on blue runs for a week doing sloppy turns and listening on their smart phones. Please don't think I have anything against sloppy turns; it's just that if you are going to become a better skier, you must be able to do some precision turns as well, and this *does* involve effort!

Fitness then is obligatory. You don't have to be pumping ninety kilos on the pec deck and running seven minute miles with a lump of lead strapped to each ankle, but it is a good idea to complete a regular and disciplined programme before you go off into the blue white yonder or Scotland etc.

You should do something to increase your aerobic capacity, ie your puff, and some anaerobic work to improve your leg, thigh, and stomach muscles. Running up and down hills, or just walking hard up and down them, is good for both puff and strength. If you can't always do this, a course at the gym on weights, combined with the aerobic machines, would be a good plan.

If you already have your own methods stick to them; there's nothing worse than doing recommended exercise that you hate when you have adequate alternatives of your own. Golf and speed chess, however, are not much use. It's worth remembering that for all the work you do getting fit, the first day or two at six thousand feet may make you feel that the effort has been wasted. Fear not. The effort will be worth it; just think of how you will feel with all those little red blood cells coursing through your veins the first morning back at the office.

I know I'm being a spoil sport now, but try not to drink too much alcohol while lunching on the mountain. It may do wonders for your relaxed mental attitude, which I mention again, but it will very quickly nullify any physical fitness, and combined with your new aggressive attitude to skiing may turn you into something very dangerous. Being breathalysed on a ski slope could also be quite embarrassing. Of course there are exceptions; if the weather has turned foul there is nothing better than getting legless in a cosy mountain restaurant with good company, a blizzard raging outside, and a ride down in the cable car just as the moon comes up.

1B – BASIC CONSIDERATIONS

STYLE & BALANCE

People often say to me 'Can you teach me to have more **style**?', and I have to reply 'Don't come to me pal, I'm as stylish as the hunchback of Notre Dame'. I've never gone much for style really. Style can go jump in the lake as far as I'm concerned. You can have *a* style of your *own*. In fact everyone develops their own *individual* style from pig ugly to amazingly beautiful (the second type being restricted to the fairer sex) without much thought, but there are people who spend a lot of time *trying* to develop it, and a lot of people who believe that to attain it will improve their performance. Off the slopes in the night club this is indeed the case, but not on the slopes. Sometimes you see the odd person coming down towards the restaurant. 'Isn't Hugo a beautiful skier?' says someone on the next table. Here he comes with his legs locked together in a pink shantung Versace suit. His arms are held out ever so slightly from his body, as he does perfect linked turns, his skis flat on the smooth piste. Put him in the bumps after a three course lunch, a bottle of wine and three pear schnapps, and I'd like to see how stylish he is then.

Did Franz Klammer have style? Not the sort of style that can be taught he didn't. No, forget about style.

You are going to sacrifice style on the high alter of better balance!

There are several ways to improve your **balance** but no short cuts to perfecting it. Balance depends on a combination of mileage, at what age you started to ski, and whether you have done any similar sports that involved balancing such as cycling or riding horses. If you started as a very young child, your balance will have come naturally, and there will be no concept of skiing being 'easy' or 'difficult'. If you started later in life, your balance will not become second nature until you have skied a very long way. You will have to rely on muscle power and fitness to hold you up and hold you steady at the start. This reliance will decline as your balance improves. What also helps considerably with your balance is thinking about where your weight is at any given moment and the type of snow you are skiing on. This is discussed in detail later.

To improve your balance **try keeping your skis about four inches apart**, rather than trying to keep them together. I don't care how close the instructor has his skis. He is only trying to look stylish. It may be a little tricky keeping the skis parallel to start with as they sometimes tend to cross, but they will soon grow out of this. **Get a little lower down too**. I was always a strong advocate of the English Lavatory Position (ELP) for those who want to use it as it lowers your centre of gravity, and gives you a wider stance, rather like a low slung, wide wheeled sports car. I am not saying that this position is obligatory for everyone during the learning process, but it does seem to suit some people. Be aware of it

The wider stance also gives you more latitude with your centre of weight which can swing to a certain extent between the two skis. I discuss this in more detail under the heading 'The Uphill Ski' (ch10).

Concentrate on keeping your weight right in the middle of your feet unless told otherwise. As you have probably never thought about where your weight is on your feet even off skis -

after all it's not something anyone spends a lot of time thinking about - try experimenting now. Just stand up with your knees a little bent and rock slowly backwards and forwards. It's quite a strange thing to do – ball of the foot, instep, heel, and back to ball of the foot – not far, but it can make a lot of difference to your balance while skiing.

Keeping your weight right on the middle of your feet therefore gives you a wider margin for error before your fore and aft balance goes, your **longitudinal balance**, and lowering your upper body by bending your knees and hips, lowers your centre of gravity to give you a more stable **lateral balance**.

You will have gathered that if you are tooling around in this mode, style will no longer be uppermost in your mind, but the more miles you put under your skis, the sooner your skis will start coming together, and the more upright you will become. In short, your *own* personal style will improve but it should be an unconscious progression.

You can improve your balance by doing a fairly simple exercise at any time during the year. Every time you do your regular pre-skiing exercise routine why not spend ten minutes trying to walk along something narrow? I used a post and rail fence in the garden. The top rail was about an inch and a half wide and thirty feet long. It was only three feet above the ground, so I didn't do too much damage when I fell off, which was quite often. I certainly improved my balance on the post and rails, but I can't be *certain* whether my ski balance improved! This is something that needs a bit more evidential proof before writing it in stone, but I *felt* it was doing some good - especially to the leg muscles.

I recently met someone for the first time who was doing t'ai chi. After an hour of tuition I suddenly realised that this ancient form of Chinese ritualistic exercise was *just* the thing to improve balance. It is especially useful as we get older and the ligaments and muscles which help us to stand up weaken naturally; t'ai chi encourages them to keep on working. **It also gives us an understanding of where our body is in the space around us**, and I found it strangely invigorating - both physically and mentally. A course with a tutor is obligatory, preferably one to one until the moves have been learnt, and then you can go it alone or in a class of fellow t'ai chi'ers.

FALLING

'How do you mean – learn to ski? One just skis or one falls over – it's as simple as that!' Ian Fleming, creator of James Bond, 1928

Obviously the high mileage you are clocking up skiing is going to mean that initially you will be **falling** a lot more. This may be bad for your ego and street cred, but at this stage in the new learning progress you will have to abandon them.

Falling is a critical part of the learning process. It helps to reduce fear, and strangely enough often reduces injury if done properly! You must learn to relax; if you tense up as you fall you will hurt yourself far more. You normally fall when you go over your limit, and if you are developing a more positive attitude to skiing, this will happen often.

Accept that you are going to fall a lot and you will learn to relax while you are doing it.

Never despair because you are falling too much! There will be off days when you are always falling and can't ski at all. You must accept it. Even the best skiers do it. They usually take the rest of the day off and go home and read a good book like this one.

If you have time to think of it, try to fall backwards with your backside dropping uphill from your skis and *relax* while you are doing it. If you can remember to keep your feet together as well, this will help too. This may be obvious to most people but it is surprising how many people fight it and end up in the most awful tangle. A fast, controlled lie down with both skis in the air can be the most satisfying fall, as it's possible to get straight back up and everybody watching thinks you have just performed your favourite trick.

After you have notched up a few hundred falls (some of which you will class bad crashes), I have no doubt that you will be controlling most of the falls and some of the crashes. You must accept that the rest of the crashes may cause injury - that is the nature of the sport – and I discuss this in more detail later.

BODY POSITIONS

As a general rule a better skier's upper body, including his head, should face down the hill. The reason for this is not as obvious as you may have been led to believe. No doubt your teachers have made you face down the hill before, and you might have thought that this was solely to prevent you from facing *up* the hill and stop you from doing all those interesting things like backwards snow ploughs and skis crossing at the back etc. You would be right to assume this, but it is only the half of the reason.

Here is an example to show why your body should face down the slope. For now treat it as a purely theoretical experiment. By all means try it if you don't believe me, but for now just imagine you are doing it.

Find a good friend and go hang him from a tree branch by his arms, so that his skis are perhaps six inches off the ground. Now get the tips of both skis and move them round so that they are at right angles to your friend's line of sight, or until he screams. His head and most of his upper body should still be facing forwards. If you let go of the skis (make sure you get out of the way quickly), the skis will swing back of their own accord to their original position. In this weightless state they swing back quite simply because of the tension in the muscles and tendons of your friend. The thigh and stomach muscles, and the tendons holding him together are wound up like a rubber band, and so long as the skier's body is facing down the hill, a turned ski will tend to swing back in the same direction when unweighted. Simple isn't it?

I said earlier that as a general rule the upper body should always face downhill, but there are a few occasions when it doesn't matter, and one or two occasions when it is even beneficial to face uphill.

For example, it is quite in order for your upper body to be facing your ski tips when tooling along on a fast traverse, or on a path, or going straight down the fall line without turning. Perhaps you are searching for goats high up above you as you tool along, but you *must* be aware that, depending on your speed, the slightest twist of your upper body, and even your hands and your head, can affect the direction of your skis.

As I have said, at the start of some long fast turns it is even beneficial to turn the upper body ever so slightly *into* the slope. This movement involves little more than bringing the downhill arm up across the chest, but it has the remarkable effect of sliding the tail of the skis round. It is like a miniature christie stop in preparation for the next turn. This action, known as contre virage, is explained later (ch7) but again demonstrates the torsional springlike power the muscles and other bits of your body can have on the skis' direction. You may have seen old film footage of skiers coming down hills before the war, where they did an exaggerated contre virage into the slope before the turn, and then twisted their upper bodies round in the opposite direction with a hurling movement of their outside arm. The long heavy wooden skis of the time readily came after their owners, like obedient dogs.

Try hurling your upper body around sometimes to start a turn without any unweighting or steering, and see what happens. The skis should follow. You will get a few funny looks, but after all the other silly things you will be doing to become a better skier, who cares?

ANGULATION

Let's now take a look at the four dangly bits - the arms and the legs. A key word here is **angulation**, and that means almost what it says, ie a bending of the hips and the knees. Its main purpose is to put the skis on their edges. This is done by bending the knees (the lower one more than the upper one), in towards the slope, and lowering the upper body by bending at the hips. It is generally done so that the weight stays over the middle of the feet and over the bottom ski, but not always. Varying degrees of angulation will be used to put the skis on their edges mostly in the turns, and by the time you have been doing this for a day or two, you will be glad that you read about fitness! Your muscles and ligaments are going to be well exercised.

ANTICIPATION

When you angulate, your upper body may be facing the ski tips, or facing down the hill, or maybe somewhere in between, depending on the type of turn you are doing. What governs your upper body position, and to a certain extent how much you angulate, is what you do with your poles. Where you put your poles to get your upper body in the right position is called **anticipation**. I *also* take anticipation to mean full use of your **eyes**, and the sensitivity of your **feet**, and I'll elaborate on that shortly.

POLE PLANT

Whenever I mention a **pole plant** the rule is that it should be made vertically unless stated otherwise. This means that it can go into the snow anywhere on the downhill side in a quadrant radius of about 2 feet from your lower boot. The further away from you it goes into the snow, the more you will need to angulate.

In my reckoning the pole plant is very nearly the most important thing for the better skier to concentrate on when learning new technique. Everything follows from it, but more later. So running through the process once again:

You must *anticipate* a turn by going down to put the pole into the snow vertically. Most of your weight will be over the middle of your lower foot. *Angulation* will get the skis on to their edge, and by so doing, will give you more precise control in the turn. You will then be in a position to set up for the next one if necessary. The speed at which you do all this depends on the type of turn you are making.

How you use your *eyes* and the *soles of your feet* is also a part of anticipation. You need to know what you are skiing on, and what you are about to ski on, so that you can react accordingly. You therefore need to be looking far enough ahead for the speed you are going, so that you can make the right decision. The feel for the snow you are skiing on comes through the soles of your feet, and tends to come with mileage and experience. It is quite an interesting exercise though to close your eyes for some seconds every now and again (preferably on a wide open, slow and empty piste) just to feel through your feet. This is discussed in more detail in the section on snowcraft.

EDGING AND CARVING

In the section about reverse camber I mentioned that the ski is designed as a spring. Depending on its construction, a ski can be bent to produce a substantial arc of reverse camber. For example, if a racer is making tight turns on ice through slalom gates, he will want the skis to be bent to their maximum to carve an arc round the gate with the minimum of sliding. On the easy gates near the finish, where the turns are little more than wiggles, he will just set the skis on their edges, with minimum reverse camber. **Edging** is just setting the ski on its edge, whilst **carving** is applying the sort of pressure to make the ski bend more than the *minimum* reverse camber. To achieve maximum reverse camber a skier does not just apply his weight to the middle of the ski, but sometimes to the front of it, by moving slightly forward at the start of a turn. This tends to bend the front of the ski first, and the bending process is amplified and transmitted back along the ski.

This is a good time to expand on something else I mentioned in the section on reverse camber. If a ski is put on its *edge* then it will have more spring in it than if the ski remains *flat* on its sole. It will also have the potential for even more reverse camber and therefore more spring. A ski flat on the snow has no potential for any reverse camber at all and that means no spring to help you into the next turn.

An edged ski will also make a much more *controlled* turn than a flat ski could ever do. Just imagine that you are on ice. Will your control in the turn be better on a flat ski or on one where the edge cuts in? The answer is obvious. Some years ago (well actually thirty years ago) we would always prepare skis for running slalom gates by scraping the soles with a sharp metal decorators scraper *bending* it slightly as we took off some of the plastic sole. This meant that the sole of the ski ended up slightly concave. The theory was that the change from edge to edge would be quicker with less time on the flat of the ski, and therefore give more control. Even while running flat the ski would have more directional stability. Whether it worked in practice I couldn't say. All I remember doing is scraping quite a few ski soles down to the wood!

SELF ASSESSMENT

In the UK this is a euphemism that raises the spectre of the dreaded IRS - Inland Revenue and Taxation, but here it means exactly what it says, and if you'll allow me I'm going to digress for a minute.

Self assessment can be used to advantage to test your grading in every sort of activity. You ask yourself the question 'How good am I at skiing?' These are the categories you can choose. They are definable enough to avoid cheating and giving yourself a better grading, or as is often the case, giving yourself a lower grading out of modesty!

Unconscious Incompetence
Conscious Incompetence
Unconscious Competence
Conscious Competence
The Zone

The 'conscious' refers to your brain and the 'competence' has to do with your body. The 'zone' is to do with nirvana and total enlightenment.

Think about them. The first stage of **Unconscious Incompetence** is that of a complete beginner. Do you remember what it was like? You hadn't a clue what you were doing and what you did do was more than likely a disaster. You were being told to do things by an instructor or a friend, but your brain was in melt down. If someone had asked you what the time was while you were trying to execute a manoeuvre, more than likely you wouldn't even hear them. Basically, you hadn't a clue what you were doing, and what you were doing you were doing badly. Anyway you didn't really care did you because it was such FUN.....wasn't it?

The next stage of **Conscious Incompetence** is where I reckon most people are. On really good days they may occasionally move into the next stage for brief moments, but are unable to harness this sudden improvement. Most of the time they are painfully aware of their shortcomings but cannot find a way to develop their technique. They know what's wrong but can't correct it. It is often an extremely frustrating stage, and it is mainly to those people that this book is addressed.

Stage three is like lifting off for the first time in an aeroplane. I don't know how it works but my does it feel good from where I'm standing. **Unconscious Competence** is a wonderful first time experience if you are a skier, and like a lot of other things you will probably remember the first time forever. Feeling the skis throwing you from one turn to another on short swings is exciting. The fact that you don't really know or don't really *care* how you do it puts you into this transitional category.

Conscious Competence is an enjoyable hard working roller coaster that takes you forward two steps and backwards one. You can start to look at skiing from the outside and begin to *feel* what it's all about. It is hard work; you start to put a lot more effort into preparing for a ski trip, understanding how the ski works, wondering why it is easier to ski on different snow surfaces, and computing and filing into your sub conscious the methods you are using to ski on them. This book should help you get well into conscious competence!

What it can't do is tell you how to get into the **Zone**. This is something that can't be taught but is the *result* of everything you've learnt and it doesn't come often. It's your moment when everything goes so perfectly - the bright sun shining out of an azure sky on to the dazzling snow, a smell of pine and wood smoke on the crystalline air - and you ski the most perfect run, every turn part of a dream to remember!

Right, that's enough, let's go for some reversion technique.

2 – REVERSION TECHNIQUE

Do you remember what it was like the first time you put skis on? Can you remember the first few days of bruises, excitement, and the thrill of uncontrolled speed? I have tried to remember how our instructor got us going but without much luck. I remember his name, and how much he drank at lunchtime, and that he had a very red face in the afternoons, but not much else. If you started a long time ago you probably won't remember a great deal either, so prepare for reversion therapy! If you started only a short time ago then all this will be instantly familiar.

This section deals with the technique that got you going up to the parallel turn. It is intended as revision so that you can revert to practising it, and thinking about how it works. This will be quite easy as you should have no longer have any restrictive influences such as fear, or badly fitting boots (like you did when you started). It will also give you an idea of how to teach a beginner. It is *not* for a beginner to use as a manual prior to skiing for the first time, as nothing can do the early learning process justice except to go out onto the slopes and experience the pleasure, terror, and mere sensation of gliding over snow for the first time. I have mentioned elsewhere some very basic guidelines for teaching, so if there is good reason to teach a friend, then *do* refer back to them.

You really *must* practise these basic techniques yourself; they will not take a long time to get through – perhaps you can run through some of them in an idle moment waiting for your friends at the bottom of the gondola. They will definitely give you an insight into where your weight is over the skis, what you are doing to steer them, and how you are unweighting them before a turn – useful things to store away for later.

THE START

Putting the skis on. Walking around on the flat to feel the skis. Running straight down on the gentlest slope to a natural stop for perhaps 20 metres. Side stepping with small steps to get back up the hill (going a little higher each time). Running straight down again taking step turns to change direction. These exercises should be done without poles.

THE SNOWPLOUGH (Stem or Wedge)

Getting into the snowplough position with the help of the poles. Alternatively, the teacher, running backwards, may hold the tips of the skis to start with. This exercise allows the skier to slide down the slope alternating between braking snowploughs, and straight running. Poles can be held, but the arms should be down by the skier's side, nice and relaxed. The knees should be slightly bent.

THE SNOWPLOUGH TURN

This basic turn can be done with or without poles at the start. By leaning over on to one ski while moving in the snowplough position, the weighted ski will turn. The weight is then transferred to the other ski to turn in the opposite direction. It should be emphasised that the weight remains on the outside ski until the next turn, ie the skier gets a feel of continually weighting the downhill ski.

SECRETS OF BETTER SKIING

Different instructors use different verbs to describe the snowplough steering action, but the instruction and demonstration must be as simple as possible! I demonstrate with an exaggerated upper body lean over on to the outside ski, sometimes bringing my hand down on to my thigh to point it out, and say 'Steer the ski round'. Others may say, 'Drive the ski round', or 'Push on the outside ski'. One of these will usually work, but there are two problems to look out for.

The first is that the skier tends to transfer his weight back on to the uphill ski as soon as the outside downhill one has made the turn. He then either sits down or else the newly weighted uphill ski slides over the middle of his downhill ski, and he falls flat on his face.

We have all done it and it may indeed happen to you at a later stage when, for example, you are skiing the bumps. It is usually sceptical apprehension rather than fear at this stage, as the brain refuses to believe that the correct inclination is for the upper body to lean out and down the hill. It usually irons itself out after a bit of mileage, and quite often only happens when turning one way. This is due to one hemisphere of the brain being more dominant than the other, or something like that.

The second problem is not as serious but can lead to worse faults later. The body is temporarily frozen into a catatonic state with arms akimbo, and poles pointing rigidly skywards or in some other direction. The skier must be encouraged to hold his hands loosely by his side. The rest of his body should then follow suit and relax.

As he skis faster there will be less weight needed on the steering ski. It is most important to chose the slope carefully. It should be wide and gentle with as few people on it as possible.

Just in case you can't wait till you have read my later advice on how to instruct a beginner and want to experiment with these turns on a victim now then please remember this:

Instructions should be minimal, and it should be remembered that demonstration will usually have more effect on a beginner's progress than the spoken word.

It is especially important not to increase the confusion in a beginner's brain, as that will be happening quite naturally already as he tries to come to terms with his strange predicament!

THE STEM TURN

The early learning process has been developed to produce order out of chaos. The various stages of turning methods have been compartmentalised into specific manoeuvres - the Snowplough, the Stem Turn, the Stem Christie, and the Parallel Christie.

Most instructors realise fairly early in their careers that chaos and confusion usually dominate beginners' thought processes, and a regimented structure of teaching does not always achieve the desired results. Indeed, some pupils need no instruction at all. I once took two thirty-year-old beginners in the Austrian Alps. I was struggling with the clips on one pupil's boots when the other impatiently decided to ski off alone. He wobbled down the slope in a semi crouch, flailing a bit with his arms, in a reasonable imitation of a Snowplough. By the time he had mastered the chairlift (about five minutes), he had crashed though the Stem Turn barrier and was doing an acceptable Stem Christie, which he has maintained for the past fifteen years.

The fact that he was my brother probably had something to do with his impatience, but it had taken me three days as a beginner in the ski school to get to the stage he had reached in less than an hour, without a word of instruction!

I appear to be digressing but the point is that our intrepid snowploughing beginner does not necessarily need to be bothered with the specific stages if his technique, however crude, appears to be advancing naturally. He may already be doing a wishy washy Stem Turn.

The Stem Turn involves little more than sliding the uphill unweighted ski in to being roughly parallel with the weighted downhill ski after a turn. The uphill ski is slid in after the downhill ski has crossed the fall line (the steepest part of the slope), and it enables the skier to experience traversing without having to do it in the snowplough position. The weight must be kept on the lower ski at all times, and this should be encouraged as there will still be a tendency for the skier to lean back and into the hill. He may also be lifting the inside ski in to join the other; this is no bad thing as it forces him to put his weight on to the lower ski, and will probably change to a slide in due course.

THE STEM CHRISTIE

The Stem Christie combines a stem and a christie, would you believe, the christie bit involving a little unweighting and bringing the skis parallel for the *majority* of the turn. The stem is used to start the turn, and *before* reaching the fall line the unweighted ski is slid in parallel to the other to provide the christie finish. At the start of the turn a pole plant is usually incorporated in order to germinate the seeds of anticipation, angulation, and a minimal unweighting movement.

SIMON DEWHURST

From a traverse the outside ski is moved into the stem position. At the same time the skier bends slightly at the knees and hips and plants the opposite pole just back from the tip of his inside ski. As the weighted stemmed ski approaches the fall line the skier rises up. The inside ski is brought in parallel as the skier rises up. At his stage the turn becomes a christie as the initially stemmed ski has now become partially unweighted by the up movement. It continues to turn across the fall line, and from his somewhat upright stance the skier drops down again for the next pole plant.

This is the theory, but in practice it is quite difficult to combine a pole plant with one side of the body and a stem with the other. If the pupil finds it too difficult, the pole plant can be passed over until practising the Christie and Christie stop.

There is, however, a major problem with the Stem Christie as a skier can become a victim of its very success. It is a reasonably uncomplicated turn to master in its basic form without a pole plant, ie just a quick stem to get the ski started in the turn, and a sliding in of the inside ski soon after. Once mastered in this form it becomes the mainstay of most skiers' repertoire. As the mileage increases, the upper ski will slide in almost immediately after a minimal stem has started to turn the lower ski. It then looks like a parallel (christie) turn. Even if a pole plant has been learnt at the start it is soon discarded, as there is no technical reason to plant the pole because the weighted ski is being steered round with a stem. Once the pole plant has been dispensed with, there is no angulation, which means less work, and a skier can quite happily spend the rest of his life tooling down well groomed pistes in the sunshine without a care in the world apart from being late for the lunchtime rendezvous.

The Stem Christie *should* be the end of the beginning, and the aim of this book is to convert some of the thousands of skiers who may have been using it for years to the exciting world beyond.

THE CHRISTIE OR PARALLEL TURN

This is the final turn that most beginners learn. Although not used a great deal by people who have discovered the Bog Standard Stem Christie and stuck to it, it is nevertheless excellent grounding for more advanced technique. Its simple difference to the aforementioned turn is that there is no stem. The skis are parallel all the time and are unweighted by a slow down and up quick motion.

There are three preliminary exercises. The first is the parallel traverse with the skis alternating between flat running with the skier standing upright, and slight angulation into the slope to put the skis on their edges. This is quite difficult for a beginner, but gives him the feel of the snow sliding under the skis as he goes both sideways and forwards with the flat running, and a basic feel of edging when he angulates. If the edging is too difficult it can be overlooked at this stage.

The second exercise is the christie stop, which involves a slow straight run down the fall line. The skier angulates directly over the skis as he goes down to put the pole in, and comes up around the pole. The pole plant, which is important, goes in between the front of his boot and the tip of the ski, thereby encouraging him to get his weight forward at the start of the turn. As he turns across the fall line the skis brake by side slipping on the snow. Plenty of weight is kept on the lower ski. This should also be practised on the other traverse.

The last exercise is alternate pole plants while stationary. The pole plant is crucial; it makes the skier go down and come up in order to unweight the skis. Some teachers also try to make their pupils jump the backs of the skis off the ground as they come up. It is quite energetic and hopefully does not last for long.

The parallel turn can now be tried on the move, going down to plant the pole, up and round it, and then down to plant the other pole to prepare for the next turn. A few turns should be linked together to provide a basic rhythm. The major fault is not weighting the lower ski enough at the end of the turn, as most pupils tend to lean too much towards the pole plant and somehow stay there. This should be discouraged!

There is also a tendency for the upper body to remain square over the skis. I don't consider this worth correcting until a skier begins to turn his upper body *into* the slope, although there are gurus, especially in Austria, who still advocate a definite upper body facing down the hill position even when the basic parallel is interspersed with quite long traverses. It is worth encouraging a skier to keep his uphill ski a few centimetres in front of his downhill ski on a traverse as this does discourage the upper body from turning *inwards*.

This then is the early learning process. Hopefully it has reminded you what it was like at the start, and given you some idea of what you are doing now. By analyzing the basic movements learnt by a beginner, you will be well briefed for what follows.

3 – SOME THEORY & EXERCISES

I once spent two weeks with a regimental ski team, who were training for the British Army Downhill Championship, in Champery, Switzerland. There's nothing very interesting about that, you may say, but two of the five soldiers taking part had only been skiing for six weeks! The competition was a week later, and these two completed the course at speeds of up to 60 mph, and they weren't last. How did they do it? They managed because they were extremely fit, they were prepared to clock up an enormous mileage, and they had a really positive attitude. Yet without being taught more than a snowplough at the start of the six weeks, they were able to ski in a downhill.

Cynics may say that their aptitude at the end of six weeks also had something to do with the munificence of the British taxpayer. The even more cynical among us may say that it was because they were lucky enough to avoid being sucked into the ski school system.

The point of mentioning this is to show you that technical knowledge is not everything, and with complete dedication to the three main principles of **fitness**, **mileage**, and **attitude**, technique can come naturally over a short time. The problem of course is that it may be impossible to adopt the soldiers' dedication because of time, money, or whatever. Besides, their training schedule did only concentrate on downhill technique, and although they eventually became ski instructors, it took them a little longer to get the hang of all the other types of turn apart from downhill ones.

Modern turning techniques were developed during the late sixties by the gurus of the time, from dissecting and analysing the smallest movements of children and racers as they tore down slalom courses. George Joubert and Jean Vuarnet from France took pictures of racers with motorised still cameras, and their movements were broken down to form the basis of the turns we use today. These quite radical changes in technique went hand in hand with the improved technology in ski and ski boot manufacture, and during the past thirty years have stabilised and been adopted almost universally as the best way to ski.

In passing I do hope that what I say on these pages will provoke some argument, and not just from the theoreticians and teachers out there. I want to know what **you** think. It's one thing to stand with someone face to face on a mountainside showing them a move that they can carry out, but I have no idea whether *written* words and a few photographs are going to get the same results. Do let me know!

Right we're off. **Let's just summarise what turns are for:**

'The turns are the manoeuvres by which the skier alters his course. The good skier uses them as sparingly as possible'. Vivian Caulfield - 'Skiing Turns' 1922.

We use them to get round corners. We use them to brake and control our speed on the piste, in the bumps, on the steep, and in powder snow. These are usually short, snappy turns. We may also use short snappy turns as an alternative to ancient courting rituals or when we feel exhilarated with excess energy. On the other hand we make fast long turns on wide empty pistes, and for off piste and glacier skiing on Spring snow, or when we feel knackered and couldn't be bothered to do short snappy turns.

Our technique will be governed by the weather, the type of snow, and even our mood on a particular day. All this is obvious, but it is surprising how many people apply the only turn in their repertoire, namely the bog standard stem christie, to try and cover all these different situations. Now I don't have anything against the bog standard stem christie; it is a very useful turn, and the basis for everything that follows, but its very success as the universal turn can be a skier's undoing. For example, if he tries to use it on ice, or the steep, or in deep snow, or trying to race round slalom gates on a club day, he is not going to find it very helpful.

Quite simply you are going to forget the bog standard stem christie and start all over again. The knowledge and expertise you have gained so far will be a help, but don't consciously draw on it. We're going back to the drawing board.

HOW DO YOU TURN A SKI?

There are many ways to turn a ski, and they nearly always depend on either **unweighting** or **steering**, or as usually happens, a combination of both. (There is also a third alternative, where you lie down on your back in the snow, swivel both skis around in the air, and your bottom too, and you find you are facing the other way when you stand up.)

UNWEIGHTING - 1 'THE DOWN SLOW & UP QUICK' METHOD

You go down slowly, and then jump the backs of the skis up. As they unweight, you can get them round. The jump becomes minimal once you have got the hang of it, and the faster you go, the less you have to unweight the skis. By the time you read this, you should be well past this stage, and will probably be doing very little unweighting. This method of unweighting is used when learning parallel turns, doing linked short turns in deep snow, and by downhillers and giant slalom skiers with slight variations.

UNWEIGHTING - 2 'THE DOWN QUICK & UP QUICK' METHOD

If you drop down on the skis towards the end of a turn they will actually unweight and come off the ground. If you don't believe me, stand on a weighing machine (preferably without skis and boots unless you have a large bathroom), and drop down very quickly. The dial will drop to zero before it comes up again to register more than your normal weight. As you drop down quickly while finishing the turn, the skis become unweighted, they slide round a little further (rather like a miniature christie stop). The weight on the skis goes back up again as you rise up and brake against the snow, the skis should follow, and you jump them up and round. This is a far more effective method than the first for certain turns, but it is harder work. It is used by slalom racers, flash Harrys on the piste, and on hard steep slopes off piste. You will also be doing it once you have digested 'The Basic Short Turn' technique. Do not worry if you do not understand this method just yet; it will be made clear later.

UNWEIGHTING - 3 THE MOGUL OR BUMPS METHOD

The bumps unweight the skis for you. As the middle of the skis pass over the top of a bump, both the back and the front of the skis come off the snow, or at least will be only lightly touching it. The skis can therefore be pivoted round on their centre points, if you do certain other things as well that are discussed in 'Better Bumps Technique'. This method, surprise, surprise, is restricted to the bumps, and is invaluable for learning to ski on them with confidence.

These are the three methods of changing the skis direction by **unweighting**, ie: lifting one or both of them off the snow. In the first two methods it is the back of the skis that are generally unweighted, and in the bumps method it is the front, or the front and the back with weight remaining over the middle.

STEERING

All turns involve steering too, some begun with an unweighting movement, and some using steering only. **Steering** involves putting weight *on* to a ski to start it turning.

Depending on the type of turn, a ski can be steered on its edge (edging and carving), and on its sole (sliding). You will probably have gathered that steering a ski on its edge involves angulation and quite a bit of work, whereas steering a ski on its sole means that you can stand more upright and relax. What usually happens is a lot of sliding and not much edging with novices, and a lot of edging and not much sliding with Alberto Tomba. As a rule novices rely on steering to make the complete turn, while more advanced skiers will unweight the skis to start the turn, and steer them to finish it off.

Just watch a few hundred skiers coming down the homebound freeway of an evening. Make a note of how they are turning. If the slope is quite testing they will be using many combinations of steering and unweighting. See if you can spot who is doing what. Don't count that fat lady in the lilac jump suit who has taken her skis off, and is walking down.

4 – PRACTICAL WORK

LEARNING POSITIONS

What you are now going to learn about now is how to maximise the skis potential by getting them on to their edges. The turns and the exercises in this section, therefore, will provide the basis for every type of controlled turn.

To learn new techniques I often suggest quite strange positions - the ELP (English/Global lavatory position), combined with a wide stance – being obvious examples. There are others like the exaggerated pole plants and angulation over the skis. These should not be adopted permanently, and with time and mileage will hopefully disappear to be replaced by a naturally acquired elegance that you can only fantasise about just now.

Their importance to start with, however, is *paramount* and will make learning so much easier.

EDGING EXERCISES

Just a few points before we start. If you have downloaded 'The Secrets of Better Skiing' from the internet it will be tricky to take these instructions up on to the mountain. With this in mind I have made them as simple as possible. Reading them through a few times should give you a basic idea of what to do.

You could always print the pages off one by one and take them with you in an inside pocket, or perhaps you could take your lap top up top.

Throughout this book I spend a lot of time repeating certain things. This is intentional as some instructions are *so* important that with only one or two mentions you may forget them.

If you have read and understood the section on edging and carving in Basic Considerations, you will recall that a ski has to be put on its edge to turn effectively in a controlled manner. The ski also needs pressure applying to its middle to make it bend into a useful reverse camber position, although this is something that will come naturally with plenty of mileage and is not a major concern here.

Let's get on to the practical stuff. These exercises are an introduction to edging, and getting a feel for the control that edging will give you before we start doing proper turns.

Tool up to a nice wide open blue run with nice white snow on it where you can go fast enough without worrying.

Are you there, or has the lift broken down again? Stand sideways against the fall line. Look down at your skis. Are the soles flat on the slope? If they are, you should find a slightly steeper slope so that the edges are cutting into the surface while you are standing virtually upright.

While standing there, lower yourself over the bottom ski as if to do up a boot buckle.

As you go down you should be aiming to touch the *middle outside* of the lower boot. Are you touching it yet? Go on, lower! Notice what has happened to the lower ski. It is even further onto its edge now. To get to this position you have had to bend your **lower knee** into the slope, and to a certain extent your uphill one too. You have also had to flex at the hips. This is **angulation**, and is an exaggeration of what you will be doing at the end of each turn shortly.

(Some teachers call this position in *motion* as 'driving the skis around'.)

Having practised this exercise at a standstill on the other traverse as well, you can now have a go at the next exercise, which you may have done before, but without having a clue why you were doing it.

Start moving slowly across the slope on your favourite traverse.

As you traverse across the slope slowly go down to touch your lower boot as you did in the standing position. This will edge the skis and put most of the weight on the lower one. This exercise whilst moving is somehow more difficult than it sounds here; doing it standing still is easy. The brain finds it a bit more difficult to accept a *moving* ski on its edge for the first time, but persevere and it will come.

Now stand up, keeping the weight on the lower ski, and you should find that the skis are sliding forwards and sideways on their soles, ie: *flat* on the snow.

Go down again to touch your lower boot. Your knees should be angulating into the slope so that your weight can remain *central* over your lower boot. Stop, turn, and do the same thing on the other traverse. While you are touching your boot there should be no sliding at all, and if the snow is right, you can look back and see the smooth, slightly curved trench that the edges have made.

A LONG CONTROLLED TURN

That gets rid of the exercises. Now for a proper turn. Tootle off on a left traverse as though you are going to do a right turn first. Start off with your right hand half way down to touching your boot. Without moving your body from this position, lift your right arm up roughly horizontally and plant the pole in the snow. This is actually little more than a momentary stab in the snow approximately as far in front of your boot as your outstretched arm will allow and only a few inches away from your downhill ski. *As* you put the pole in start to rise up. Rise up fast enough to unweight the back of the skis with a parallel turn so that you can start to bring them round. There is no need for the backs of the skis to come right off the ground; in fact it is important to apply as little unweighting as possible in your upward movement to maintain control. The faster you go the easier it will be to unweight the backs of the skis.

You will speed up as you go into the fall line. Come round as smoothly as possible, and drop down slowly as if to touch the left boot with the left hand this time. At the same time apply pressure on to the lower ski. By 'applying pressure' I mean that you should have a sense of pushing hard down on to the ski with your leg and thigh muscles into the middle of your foot. It should feel as though you are *driving* the skis round, and the whole movement must be done smoothly and firmly.

Why should you apply pressure in this way? Well eventually with more speed and less unweighting this downward pressure will start pushing the skis into added reverse camber, which as you probably remember will make them carve through the turn and because they are bending under tension they will give you a spring to bounce you into the next turn as you start unweighting once more.

(You will notice I have put the phrase 'applying pressure' into inverted commas. This explanation would not stand up in physics, but you will understand what I mean when you start doing it. There must in fact be a *weighting* of the lower ski as you come round after the slow upward *unweighting* movement, and coupled with the turning action of the ski on its edge, a satisfactory reverse camber can be achieved.)

The skis must not be rushed around as you come into the fall line, and from above their tracks should resemble a nicely rounded capital S once you have done a turn on the other traverse. As you come round after this first turn and *start* to angulate, the inside edge of the lower ski will *start* to bite. Carry straight on and come up after putting the left pole in, speed up into the fall line, and once again go down smoothly and firmly. Do a few more before stopping, and if you haven't got the hang of it, stop, think about it, and start again.

Compare the difference between the two sequences. The first turn will make a large capital S on the snow and the skis, because they are on their edges for most of the turn, will give excellent snow holding and control. In the second sequence I have rushed round coming to the fall line in a near standing position and the skis for the most part remain flat with little edging.

You will find to begin with that you may be sliding more on the soles of the skis than carving on the edges, but as you learn to angulate more, and apply more pressure to the lower ski, it will start to bite. There is obviously a section of the turn as the skis come into the fall line and pass it when they are flat on the snow transferring from one edge to the other. This is the part of the turn when it is most difficult to maintain a nicely rounded S. You should make a positive effort to let the skis come round smoothly even while they are sliding flat on the snow. Incidentally, it is virtually impossible to carve a turn 100% with *no* sliding, but should you feel like a challenge perhaps you could be the first person to do it.

There are two important things to remember when trying out this turn. The first is to avoid a common fault. When most people turn into the fall line and start to speed up, they tend to rush the turn round in order to brake as quickly as possible and slow themselves down again (see the photo sequence). This tends to make things worse rather than better, and it's therefore important to accept and allow this increase in speed.

If you want to build more confidence in this respect find a steep bit of piste leading to a flat or uphill gradient. Practise running straight down the steep bit after a final turn, knowing that you will be able to stop easily. Don't you just love that feeling of acceleration with the wind in your hair, and your eyes watering so much that you can't see where you are going?

The second point is to make sure that your upper body, from the hips up, is facing down the hill *as much as possible*. Rather than make a positive effort to face down the hill at this stage (after all you have a lot of other things to concentrate on), just make a point of looking for the area in front of you where you could be making the next turn. The faster you go the further ahead you should be looking. If your head is facing downhill then it is reasonable to assume that your upper body may just be as well. It's permissible for it to be *square* over the skis but at this stage *it must never face towards the hill.*

SIMON DEWHURST

SHORT (SWING) TURNS - THE STANDARD MODEL

Certain turns are for certain conditions. The long carved turns using up the whole of a wide smooth piste are for fast skiing, where braking is not a necessity. These turns are the basis for giant slalom and downhill technique.

On steep or busy slopes, however, or in the bumps, or while learning to ski in the powder, you will need to brake your speed more, so here is the basic short turn that will keep you going nicely on these surfaces in perfect control.

Go to a gentle blue piste to start with in order to concentrate on these exercises. Before you start to do anything imagine your upper body position as you drive a car. Your head is facing the front. Your arms are holding the steering wheel. They are held out, slightly bent at the elbow, in front of you. The rest of your upper body is held facing the front by the shape of the seat. This all pre-supposes that you are not trying to tune the radio or wind down the passenger window.

Stand on a flat bit of your chosen slope and assume the driving position. Face straight down the hill. Hold your arms out at chest height as though gripping the steering wheel of your sit-up-and-beg roadster. By now quite a few passers-by will have stopped to look at you.

The poles are held quite firmly, hanging down with the points just off the snow. This is the position in which your upper body *must* remain the whole time that you are moving and turning down the piste (not for ever but just for this exercise!). Your skis will be going from side to side underneath you like windscreen wipers.

SECRETS OF BETTER SKIING

Get going straight down a minimal slope jumping the skis from side to side across the fall line underneath you. This is where all that fitness training is going to come in useful.

You are travelling quite slowly, no more than five miles an hour, your body is facing the front, and your arms are held out as though gripping the steering wheel. You will find that the only way to get the skis round each time is to go down slowly, and then jump them up and across the fall line, ie a down slow and up quick unweighting. As you go down put the pole in firmly, jump up and around it, and immediately go down to put the other pole in for the next turn.

The object of this exercise is to get a rhythm going with one turn after another, and to give you a feeling of the skis going underneath you whilst your upper body stays rigidly facing the front. You will probably be wishing by now that you had never bought this book.

Have a rest after a few turns, and then try again. It will seem pretty rough to start with, especially trying to keep the skis parallel and bringing them round tidily, but worry not. While you are having a rest, try this sequence a few times standing still: down, right pole in, up ... .down, left pole in, up ... and so on.

The next time you go increase the speed a bit, remembering that the faster you go the less effort is needed to unweight the skis. Continue to do one turn after the other with no lapse in between. Hum a catchy little tune to yourself and keep in time with its beat; you should be doing about one turn a second.

Now there comes a time, and it is quite often a natural progression, where the method of unweighting the ski goes through a subtle change from down-slow-and-up-quick to down-*hard*-and-up-quick. If you drop down hard towards the end of a turn to put the pole in, the skis will unweight for an instant, allowing them to slide slightly further round against the fall line. As the weight on them increases (see p.14), and because you are angulating, the edge of the lower ski will dig into the snow. This is known as setting an edge. It is in effect a braking movement as the ski will quite often stop dead. You can then jump around into the next turn. As I say the lower ski is quite often motionless for a split second, and if the snow is soft you should be able to see the imprint made by the bottom of the ski. The tracks of these short turns will differ considerably from the large S shapes of the long turns.

There will be little carving at this stage, although later on as you clock up the mileage you should start to carve a little before setting an edge. At this early stage, however, the tracks you are making will look more like a z than an s.

To really get into the swing of doing these short turns you must introduce a bit of aggro into your performance. As you push hard down on the snow, say something aggressive to yourself like 'Hard down! Hard down!', or 'Attack! Attack!'. I remember teaching two fit girls a few years ago who wanted to be extricated from the famous bog standard stem christie. I told them to say something aggressive and skied down a few metres to watch them. The first girl came down in a rather half hearted fashion, going a bit too fast, and not driving down hard enough to brake her speed and get some turns in. I asked her what she had said to herself, and she replied 'Hard down! Hard down! Hard down!'. When the second girl got going, she was really giving it some welly, and did about twenty turns in fifteen metres, collapsing in a heap at our feet. When she had got her breath back, I asked her what magic phrase had produced such a brilliant performance, and she replied, 'Screw you, Simon! Screw you, Simon! Screw you, Simon!'.

At some stage you will mistakenly put too much weight on the uphill ski and fall over, so once you have got the hard down movements stored in the memory banks, you can say instead, 'Left ski, right ski', etc, to help keep the weight on the downhill ski as you come hard down on it.

Eventually there will come a time when you do a turn and suddenly feel the skis throwing you into the next one. You have arrived! You have applied enough pressure to bend the skis into an added reverse camber and they will have become real springs! You will also be polishing off the turn by carving a little! The skis will track round more accurately and smoothly before bouncing you into the next turn.

The pain of having splashed out all that valuable cash on a pair of performance skis will now turn to joy as you realise that it has all been worth it!

As a final exercise, and to give you something that will be completely knackering and set you up nicely for lunch, see how many turns you can do in a given distance, let's say in thirty metres. This will help your rhythm, and get you used to the braking action of the turn. It will also make you fitter, and help elasticise those natural springs, the old thigh and stomach muscles.

Remember that it is *imperative* to keep the upper body facing down the hill the whole time you are doing short turns.

Once you get the hang of doing these turns on easy open pistes, you are set up for more adventurous terrain, and for learning variations of the standard short swing turn.

SIMON DEWHURST

5 – SKIING IN THE BUMPS

For most people the bumps are to be avoided, or else treated with masochistic grit. But for the better skier they should be like a honey pot to a bear, so go and find some. If you approach bump skiing methodically, there is nothing to stop you skiing them well and with confidence within a week, and then only practising for half an hour a day.

Now that you have mastered fall line skiing, ie doing one turn after the other without traversing, you are ready to take the bumps in your stride, or whatever else you would like to take them in.

Most people want to know which part of the bump to ski over, and I tell them that **while they are learning**, they should always try to go over the top in order to maximize the unweighting potential that the bump offers absolutely free. If the bump is enormous, and you're not sure if someone is having a picnic the other side of it, then by all means take it on the side. As you become more of an expert you can start to ski in the valleys or wherever you like.

As you probably know, bumps are formed by people continually skiing in the same tracks which soon become troughs, and gradually building them up by pushing more and more snow from the troughs up to ridges.

Usually the crest of the bump, the ridge, is soft snow that has been pushed from the dip uphill from it. In the dip itself there is a lot of even softer and sometimes quite deep snow that has been scraped off the downside of the previous bump. The downsides of bumps can therefore be quite icy from people side slipping.

EXERCISE ON A BUMP

Read the following and do the exercises as slowly as you like – the slower the better so that you take it all in.

Try these following steps:

Find some well formed, nicely spaced bumps on a gentle gradient. Make sure they are nice bumps, closely grouped, and not some horrendous sausage shaped monsters with cliffs and small bushes growing out of them. On the traverse ski slowly over the top of one of these nicely spaced bumps until the middle of the boot is perched on the very summit.

Stop and think about where to put the pole in. Remember that the skis are still on the traverse. If your body is in the driving position facing down the hill (which it should be for short turns), then you will find that the pole should go in about 12" from your boot, and slightly down the far side of the bump. You will have to bend at the knees and hips with your weight in the middle of your foot on the lower ski, in order to get the pole in.

So you are now standing motionless on the top of the bump, your upper body facing down the slope, your pole perpendicular in the snow down from your boot, and your skis still on the traverse. While you are standing there, let's just go over this perpendicular pole plant again. I have already mentioned that the pole plant is a crucial part of anticipation (ch1B) and while learning to ski the bumps **it is imperative that you get it right, because everything else follows.**

If you make a definitive pole plant with the point going right into the snow, and the pole is perpendicular as it goes in, you will *have* to angulate over the skis, you will *have* to weight the lower ski, and your body will *have* to be facing down the hill.

It is quite possible that as you stand on the bump, only a foot of ski is actually touching the snow, as the back and front are both off it, or only barely touching it. Now remember what I have said about the torsional qualities of your thigh and stomach muscles (ch1B); you will immediately twig that the skis should swivel round with the slightest encouragement. Back to the exercise.

As you put the pole in, your weight will be projected slightly over the downside of the bump, the skis will tip forwards, and will start to slide round. They will probably side slip into the soft snow on the backside trough of the next bump.

Remember to keep the weight in the middle of your foot on the bottom ski. Line up another bump on the other traverse, and try it again.

Keep low and keep a wide stance throughout this exercise, because you are going from a stop into an acceleration, and then to a stop again, from soft snow to ice, and back to soft snow. Your balance could be all over the place!

LINKING TURNS TOGETHER

Now try a few bumps linked together, so instead of side slipping to a halt in the dip, keep up some forward momentum by pointing the skis more down the hill. You should almost come to a stop on the bump before dropping over it. Remember the pole plant. Gauge your speed, and use the dip with the snow in it to brake you before the next pole plant. You will have to keep a very close look at the ground; anticipate the braking trough, and the accelerating downside, and move your weight slightly backwards for the dip and slightly forwards for the downside.

This weight shift backwards and forwards needs some explanation. You will recall that as a general rule the weight should remain over the middle of your foot. Well it actually should stay over the middle of your foot, but as the gradient is continually changing, there will be an apparent shift of weight all the time. Well something like that. The main thing is to anticipate the change in gradient. It's one thing for the skis to slide out from underneath you as you sit down with a bump. It's quite another for them to stop dead on the upside of a bump catapulting you head first out of both bindings. Even after a hundred catapults I still find it embarrassing.

You may find to start with that the uphill ski crosses over the top of the downhill as you come round, thereby putting you in a somewhat tricky position. Quite often there appears to be a lot of weight on the uphill ski as it crosses over, and you stop dead and fly out of the front. As long as you project your weight forward as you put the pole in, and keep it forward until the skis have come round, you should avoid this problem as your weight will remain over the downhill ski.

This tentative exercise of linking some bumps together should be done at the start of every session for twenty turns or so to get you into a good rhythm. If you do it slowly and methodically, there is a good chance that you will complete at least one run without mishap, and at this stage you need all the confidence you can get!

SIMON DEWHURST

KNEE EXERCISE

As you start moving down the bumps a little more confidently, you will have to alter your technique slightly to absorb the uplift that they are providing. Can you imagine what would happen if you stood upright and took the bumps straight? By the eighth bump you would be wondering if you had paid your next holiday insurance, and by the twelfth you would be airborne. The next time you hit the ground could well be onto the terrace of your favourite restaurant. The secret technique to avoid this problem and prolong your good health is to bend ze knees, and use the thighs as shock absorbers, so that you can float over a mogul field like a softly sprung limousine.

As an exercise ski slowly on a traverse across some medium sized bumps. Imagine that your head is clamped in a vice that will neither go up nor down nor from side to side, ie, it will only run in a straight line above the slope. As you are moving make sure that your knees are already bent a little more than they would be on a smooth piste. You will also have to bend a little at the hips to keep the weight over the middle of the skis. This is angulation down over the skis without edging.

As you glide slowly over the bumps allow them to push your knees up even further. Keep your head steady and try to keep your weight over the middle of the skis. Do this exercise quite a few times to get the feeling of your new shock absorbers. It will be hard work on the knee joints and thigh muscles, but remember that skiing is good for you. As you come over a bump try and push the skis down into the trough so that you are in good contact with the snow for as long as possible. This angulation over the skis means that your centre of gravity is kept low. Just like the first exercises, it will be easier to keep your balance if you keep low.

You can now attack the bumps again head on. This time adopt the car driving position that you learnt for the short turns on the piste, with your hands held out slightly in front of you, and the rest of your upper body facing rigidly down the hill.

Go as slowly as you need, and allow the bumps to do the unweighting.

Keep your head steady and remain in the driving position.

Do one turn after the other to keep close to the fall line, so be on the lookout for the next bump.

Keep the weight on the downhill ski.

GETTING THE RHYTHM

As you start to get a rhythm and clock up the miles, you will not need to be so definitive with the pole plant, and eventually you will be able to dispense with it. Remember that the pole plant is intended as aid to the learning technique.

Accept the inevitable while skiing in the bumps, and that is **they will get you in the end!** You will find, psychologically, that if you are feeling on top of the world, you will also find you are on top of the bumps, and if by chance you are down in the dumps, you will be down in the bumps as well. Go for them on a nice sunny day and ski them for just a short time so that the experience sinks into your memory bank and is allowed to settle before giving it another go.

Minimize the bumps' murderous intent by choosing nicely arranged ones wherever possible, and a nice sunny day with a bit of fresh snow on the top to soften the falls. Don't go up onto the black run where those aforementioned brutes lurk, with their bottoms sheered into cliffs, just waiting to gobble you up.

If you get the chance, go and watch a bumps competition either for real or on a video. From the front the skiers' upper bodies will sometimes appear to be motionless except for their progress down the mountain. Their legs will be going like pistons underneath them. As each bump unweights the skier and tries to catapult him into space, he absorbs it with rapid angulation of his knees, which are thrown from one side of the fall line to the other. He is therefore edging slightly to brake him, but as he is skiing so close to the fall line, this braking is minimal.

The technique of absorbing the bumps in this way is known as 'avalment' from the French 'avaler', to swallow. This, in essence, is what you have been practising, and probably what you will be doing while watching him.

Points to remember while you are learning:

Keep as low as possible.

Maintain the driving position all the time.

Use the top of the bump to unweight the skis.

Anticipate the continual changes in gradient.

CHAPTER 6 – OFF PISTE

'The British off-piste skier is a great enthusiast. For him skiing is a form of arduous training, and the pleasures of the hot chocolate, the hot bath and the stiff gin are all the more intense for being well earned. Of course he likes skiing in soft powder snow but he takes the rough with the smooth more philosophically than most, and would not dream of letting bad conditions interfere with his plans. 'Often you get your best skiing in a whiteout', he will bark while doling out porridge at dawn.'
Adam Ruck - UK Sunday Telegraph 2002

POWDER SKIING TECHNIQUE

This is what it's all about - the White Stuff! No more weaving down the piste trying to avoid the crowds and the fat lady in the lilac shell suit, because this is freedom man, this is the ultimate. That's roughly how it was explained to me the first time I was encouraged to go off into the fresh powder snow. It was exhilarating, demanding, and quite unlike anything I had been used to.

Before you go off piste into the powder, you must answer this question: Are you prepared to become a complete beginner again? Yes? Well, read on. You may get the hang of it within the hour. It may take you a little longer, but as long as you read this next section carefully and slowly, and act on it, you will be able to ski the powder. **Before going out and trying it, I**

strongly recommend that you read the section on Avalanches. This is not to put you off, but rather to give you an idea of what is safe to ski and what is not.

To succeed in deep snow you must ski gently, and you must feel what you are doing. You have to be spot on with your balance, because the snow is always trying to snag the outside edges of the skis wherever you try to turn them. You seem to be stuck in tram lines, and then if you do manage to somehow turn, the tips of the skis sink down, stop dead, and throw you out of the window.

I'm going to be sexist here. Girls seem to get the hang of deep snow quicker than boys. I think the reason for this is that they are much more *gentle* with the stuff and this is one of the secrets to skiing powder. Go lightly and treat the snow with the same respect you would give to the spider you are gently fingering out of the bath tub

Now for business. The following introductory exercises are quite important, and should not be skipped.

1) Find a slope of fresh untouched snow, steep enough to run down at a steady pace. (Don't worry too much about the people coming past you with beards, shouting at you to stop spoiling their special bit of angel poop.) With your weight slightly back *and equal on both skis*, carefully bounce up and down. The skis should be about 4" apart. It should feel as if you are bouncing up and down on a trampoline, as the snow compacts on your down movement. This trampolining effect is what makes powder skiing such magic. The snow needs to be at least knee deep, otherwise you won't get the bouncing effect.

Let me just repeat where your weight should be while learning deep snow technique. It should be *slightly* back from the middle of the foot, that is towards the heel. I do not think it a good idea to encourage you to sit well back on the heels of your skis while trying to ski the deep stuff. Your skis are more liable to accelerate, and you will not be able to anticipate the next turn properly, **so forget about leaning back!** As you begin to get the hang of powder skiing your weight should move forwards to the middle of your feet.

2) Repeat this exercise, but this time do alternate left and right pole plants as you go down. Feel that your balance is right. The distance that your body goes up and down is important. As you go down to put your pole in, your head should be almost level with your hand! That's a long way down. Remember the driving analogy while doing this; keep both hands rigidly in front of you and face down the hill.

3) The next stage is to turn, so find a slope that's a little steeper. You will need a steeper slope than a groomed piste of the same gradient, as deep snow slows you down. Stand at the top and try to memorise the rhythm of the exercise you have just done. Repeat it standing still. Down, left pole in, up. Down, right pole in, up. Left pole, right pole, left pole, right pole. Remember that your body must face downhill all the time, your weight must be equal on both skis and *slightly* back towards your heels, and that the skis must remain flat on the snow. Right, off you go. Let's say you are starting with a right turn. Weight on both skis. Go all the way down to put the right pole in. Come right up, and as you come up, jump the skis across the fall line. (Keep the skis *flat* in the snow.) Now, with the same rhythm, start to go down immediately for the next turn, put the pole in, and jump up and around with the skis. Keep your body facing down the hill, keep the skis flat, keep the rhythm going (count to yourself), and go riiiiight dowwwn each time. (I haven't said it yet but you will be unweighting the skis with the 'down slow and up quick' method while you are learning. This

will eventually progress with linked turns to the 'down quick and up quick mode')

After about seven turns you may well be knackered, trying to keep perfect balance, working your knees, hips, stomach, and arms, and coupling all this with unbelievable concentration. Take a break and breathe in the rare mountain air, and listen to the silence, and think how lucky you are not to be sitting in the bank manager's office.

You will find that you get tired quite quickly because your muscles are working overtime to compensate for the difficulty of keeping your balance. It is therefore very important to think 'Balance', to think 'Rhythm', to think 'Gently'. When you are doing more headplants than turns, give it a break until you have recovered. It is a good idea to try a bit of deep snow close to the piste initially, so that you can get back on the piste and boost your deflated ego for a while. Don't do it for too long; get back into the angel poop before someone else pinches it all.

Let's just summarise the important points for learning to ski the powder:

Keep your weight **equally balanced on both skis**
(a few inches apart)

Go **right** down to plant the pole

Keep your upper body facing **downhill all the time**

Keep a **rhythm** going ie: **short linked turns** (like window wipers)

Be **gentle**

SKI THE STEEP - JUMP TURNS

Now that you have mastered the powder, nothing can damage your ego, so let's get down to some really macho stuff. How many times have you looked up at that couloir and said, 'Wish I could do that'? Conversely, how many times have you looked up at that couloir and said, 'Gosh. That scares the pants off me. Let's go for some lunch'. Well, if you have reached this point in the book without putting yourself into intensive care, you are ready to ski the steep.

Make sure the conditions are right. Generally the steepest slopes are off piste and can really only be skied successfully when the snow has melted and frozen a few times to form a firm smooth surface. The best time for this is early Spring. Choose a sunny day and check the weather forecast, the avalanche factor, and your insurance.

The time to attack the steep late in the season is early in the morning just after the top layer of snow has been softened by the sun, but not so much as to make it rotten and prone to avalanche. At first choose a wide open slope and not a couloir. This at least gives you the option of traversing out if necessary. It should be way off track, away from the distractions of all those sad piste bashers. Preferably choose a smooth slope with no rocks or trees of other miscellaneous obstacles such as chamois or marmots.

The gradient needs to be more than 45 degrees to be considered steep, and from 55 to 70 degrees to be extreme. Don't try anything more than 55 degrees to start with. The slope should be concave with a nice gentle outrun. This will mean that if you do fall there is nothing to hit on the way down, and you will come to a nice gradual stop with nothing more than a bruised ego.

SIMON DEWHURST

One of the golden rules of the mountains is never travel alone off piste, so you have to take a friend. I say 'have to' as though a friend may be an encumbrance. However, you may have gone up the mountain with the intention of having a secluded picnic among the pine trees with your best friend anyway. This bit of steep you have come across is a mere bagatelle.

To get you into the mood take a few deep breaths and admire the view. 'Oh look. Isn't that the Matterhorn over there? Let's do that after this. Oh look. There's the North Face of the Eiger. Let's do that after lunch'.

So, you have taken a few deep breaths to relax, smeared a liberal smearing of factor 90 all over exposed parts, and are now carefully traversing and side slipping into your chosen starting point. Stop. Look. Imagine the line you are going to take which should be as close to the fall line as possible. You are going to go as slowly as possible doing linked braking turns. You are going to start each turn with a perpendicular pole plant about 18" (yes, 18") down from the front of your lower ski boot. This will ensure that you get your weight well down the hill. As a general rule, the steeper the slope, the further down you should make your pole plant. This means simply that your weight is always ahead of your skis. You can imagine that if you planted the pole next to your boot, the skis would have more chance of sliding away from you as you brought them round. Your weight would then be uphill and behind your skis.

You are now standing with your skis at right angles to the fall line. They have created their own little ledges. To maintain complete control at the end of every turn, the skis will finish up in this position for an instant before the start of the next turn. Remember learning the short linked turns way back? On a gentle slope the edge sets would have made a pattern on the snow something like this:

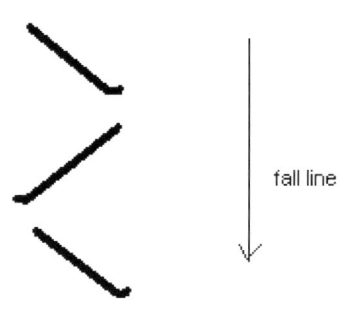

On a steep slope they will have to make a pattern more like this:

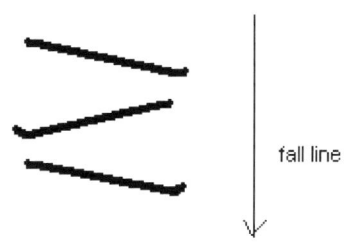

On a very steep slope the skis will be at right angles to the fall line. This position will minimize any forward slide of the skis into a traverse and will brake them. In fact you will be side slipping into the edge set, so that the side slip and the edge set combined should look more like this:

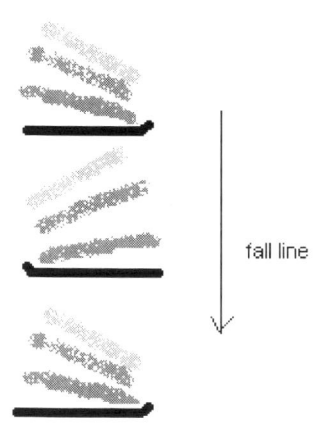

Back to the nitty gritty. You must now angulate down over your lower boot, and make the pole plant like you would in the bumps, except that it is perhaps 18" down from your boot. To get the skis around you are making a slow down and quick up unweighting. As they pass the fall line your weight will start to come down over the lower ski, and you will angulate down again to make the next pole plant. Although this will need quite an effort, it must be done as smoothly as possible.

Concentrate on keeping the skis in contact with the snow, and minimize the jump around. This will encourage a smoother braking as you start to go down for the next pole plant. Try to link five or six of these turns before stopping for a rest. Make sure the skis are braking at 90 degrees against the fall line to minimize any forward traverse. This will ensure you are moving down the mountain in a narrow corridor not much wider than the length of your skis. You will realise that your upper body is always facing down the mountain during these turns, and will help the skis to rotate a little.

When you feel confident enough you can then try that narrow couloir running under the cable car. For that particular couloir there is no need to take a friend as someone in the cable car is bound to call for the ski patrol.

There are a few important points to remember

Choose a slope free from rocks which would otherwise have to be avoided.

The best stuff to learn on is spring snow that has not had too much sun on it.

If you're some way off piste make sure you are not alone.

OFF PISTE IN THE SPRING

As the season progresses into early spring the snow conditions undergo an interesting change. Snow that was cold and powdery and crystalline because the daytime temperature stayed below zero, now turns into what most people call slush or sugar. During the daytime the sun raises the ground temperature where its rays hit the mountain, and the snow crystals break down into nothing more than blobs. This starts at lower altitudes, but as time marches on so it moves to the higher ground and eventually on to the glaciers. What interests the better skier is the quality of this stuff if caught at the right time.

Spring snow is not as exciting as powder snow, but it is wonderfully flattering. The night time temperatures continue to drop below zero, so by morning the snow is frozen solid. Given an hour or two of warm sunshine, and the top layer, perhaps an inch or so, thaws out and turns a mountainside into one naturally made prepared piste. There are no icy patches, no bumps, and no other man made obstacles. It is a very flattering surface to ski on.

High up on the glaciers the transition also takes place. Fresh snow that has fallen earlier in the year and concealed crevasse openings, now thaws and freezes many times to form solid bridges over what would otherwise be lethal man traps. This means that the glaciers can be skied early on in the day in comparative safety.

So if you decide to take a late holiday and find most of the snow in your resort base gone, pack a picnic and go ski some glaciers or anywhere else in the white blue yonder. I usually use the lift system to get as much height as possible and tend to start with the first lifts of the day.

Find out about the safety of the area before you go, and if necessary, take a large scale map. **On no account must you or your party ever attempt glacier skiing on your own without a guide unless you have thoroughly checked the state of the area or the lie of the land with qualified local knowledge.** If you are in any doubt hire a guide who is familiar with the terrain. It will cost you money, but weighed against the possibility of an expensive rescue operation should you fall down a crevasse, or even death, a guide wins hands down.

Most ski shops will rent you a pair of skins and some randonee bindings. The skins unroll and stick to the bottom of your skis. They are man made and are like bristles that will only let the skis go forward so you can walk up hills without sliding backwards. The bindings attach to the ones already on your skis, and allow your heel to come up. Once you are at the top and ready to push off they go back into your rucksack. Never try to ski down with the skins on. They can ruin a good descent!

There is not a great deal of technique to be dealt with. You should keep a wary eye out for the lie of the land, as it is still quite easy to end up in a cul de sac even with the aid of a large scale mountain map. Make sure the weather is clear and sunny with a good forecast; if the weather should close in you will be on your own. Be extra observant with looking ahead, and make sure there is nothing on the slope ahead that could be a danger. Some of the terrain will be steep, and some will be easy. Because the snow surface is so forgiving you will find it the nicest stuff you have ever skied on. So much for the difficulties of off piste!

Incidentally, sugar snow is the fastest stuff to ski on; it is thought that every blob existing in its half melted state has a layer of water surrounding it which is more slippery than snow at or below freezing. This is excellent news for speed skiers who break most of the speed records on this type of snow.

It will take a little time to judge whether the conditions are going to be suitable, so check it what I have to say about snow types.

SKI THE STEEP IN POWDER

You will only be able to ski powder on a slope up to about 50 degrees. Any steeper than this and the snow will tend to avalanche in even the most stable conditions, and then it becomes a matter of coming down on whatever base there is underneath. If you throw caution to the wind you could of course come down in the avalanche itself. As a general rule restrict the steep and deep to slopes with plenty of trees dotted around. This tends to reduce the chance of an avalanche. Trees have the added advantage of providing yet another challenge – how to get round them.

Powder on the steep is best when it is thigh to waist deep; it is more exciting, and also has a tendency to slow you down, which is no bad thing. The braking effect of the snow against your skis, legs, and thighs, or even waist, means that you don't have to come round against the fall line so much with the jump turns, and the braking movement down on the skis can be more gentle.

You will need to spread your weight more between the two skis, and it may take a little time to work a compromise between weighting the lower ski only, to weighting both skis equally. You will be looking for a compromise between easy powder skiing technique, and the slightly more aggressive technique needed for a firm steep slope.

The bouncing you do, and the depth into the snow you drop *while* you are bouncing will help to brake you. It will also determine the amount of snow that cascades up into your face and over your shoulders. Wear goggles. You'll need them. Unless you are an ace swimmer, and can get your breathing synchronised with your bouncing, keep your mouth shut, except of course to whoop with sheer joy at the fun of it all.

Quite a few people lose a ski in the deep powder. If the avalanche risk is low, it is not a bad idea to have some kind of cord fastening going round your ankle and attached to the ski. Alternatively I have often managed to keep my skis attached by diving head first down the slope when I was about to fall! It takes a bit of time to clear the snow out of exposed orifices, but it saves digging around in angel poop up to your neck, searching for a ski that has probably moled its way into the next valley.

It is also important when skiing off piste in any condition to wear or carry some kind of reflector or transmitter that will help any rescuers dig you out, should you be buried in an avalanche. On that glum note, shall we proceed?

7 – ADVANCED TURNS

LONG FAST TURNS - INTRODUCTION

I learnt to ski in a Norwegian resort where the mountains were more like steep hillocks, and the longest runs were half a mile, cutting narrow swathes through the birch trees. Short carved turns were the order of the day (and sometimes the night). Arriving in the European Alps I was amazed to find huge open pistes rolling down the mountainsides for miles. Short turns were out for the time being; long turns at speed were in.

Speed, however, is as potentially dangerous on a piste as a loaded gun in the hands of a five year old, unless we know how to use it. How many times have you been run into? How many times have you run into somebody else? How many times have you seen people totally out of control careering headlong down the mountain?

SAFETY AT SPEED

How fast do you think you ski at the moment, excluding the time you get into the tuck at the bottom of the blue run? 10, 20, 30 mph? You are probably not going much more than 30 mph, but have you thought how well you would be after hitting a tree even at this speed? Even at 30 mph you have to look out for people, rocks, and snow machines, etc, but how will you anticipate these problems at 50, 60 or even 70 mph? The fat lady in the lilac shell suit may be two hundred metres ahead, dithering, but how do you avoid her at 60 mph? It may be hysterically funny in the bar afterwards, reminiscing on how you went straight over the front of her skis in the air for God's sake, shouting 'Banzai'.

An alternative, which does happen, is that you both end up in a wooden box.

It is now standard practice in some Stateside ski resorts to breathalyse those who ski dangerously, so this suggests a direct comparison with driving a car: Be aware of your speed – Keep your distance – Watch out for others – Know your reaction time – Know your stopping distance – Reduce speed in heavy traffic. As responsible skiers we must file these comparisons away so that they become instinctive and do not need thinking about again. We can then safely apply ourselves to the technique.

For all the fast turns choose a good wide empty blue run on a Monday when the weekenders have gone home. Make sure you can see the whole piste you are going to practise on before stopping. It doesn't need to be more than 25 degrees to start with. There are no stray weekenders hiding behind those hillocks, nor snow machines chugging up round blind corners? Good. Unless it's warm put some goggles on. There's nothing worse than being blinded by tears at speed.

THE LAZY FAST TURN

Get going on a fast traverse. Your upper body can be facing the ski tips, unlike the short turns. Because you are skiing on a reasonably flat slope, there will not be the need to edge, so you will be standing almost upright with your knees slightly bent over the skis just to give a bit of shock absorption and to have your upper body in a good position for initiating the turn. This means that the skis will be virtually flat on the snow.

To initiate the turn you must now anticipate by rising into an upright position, and at the same time projecting your weight forward towards an imaginary spot about 12" to the *downhill* side of your ski tips. This projecting will do two things. First it will unweight the back of the skis, and secondly, because your body is now facing *slightly* down the hill, your natural torsion will be brought into play. As the skis come round into the fall line, apply slight pressure *forward* on the inside edge of the downhill ski. This will help you to come round more smoothly. The faster you are going the more effective will be the turn.

If you initiate the turn with a stem you are cheating.

Try to describe a perfect arc on the snow. There should be no pushing down on the back of the lower ski to get the skis round against the fall line and therefore brake them. The basic fast turn is designed to give you a feel for accelerating into the fall line. It has little or no practical use. I use it at the end of the day when I'm trying to get home quickly and haven't the energy to angulate and edge the skis into more precise turns.

This turn should not be used on a crowded piste.

Remember that your weight should always be *slightly* forward of the middle of your foot.

THE FAST TURN – EDGING

This is the same turn as before but on a steeper slope so that you can make full use of the skis' edges to give you more precise control. Choose an easy red run without too many bumps. You must provide sufficient angulation to keep the skis on their edges at all times, except when you rise to come round across the fall line. As you come round apply the pressure to the front of the down hill ski as you angulate once more. This is the basic giant slalom turn used by racers, and as long as your edges are sharp it will work for you just as well on ice as on nice stuff. Like the basic fast turn with your skis flat it is not designed with any braking in mind, as the skis are carving for the most part. While the skis are coming into the fall line, however, there is a chance that they may side slip and lose the precise control you are aiming for. To reduce this here is something really exciting - lateral projection.

GIANT SLALOM TURN & LATERAL PROJECTION

Ever since you started skiing you have been encouraged to keep your weight on the downhill ski. Now for the first time (officially) you are going to ski on your uphill ski. Try these two exercises to give you an idea of what it feels like:

1) Choose an easy gradient and traverse across it slowly, skis *flat*, with weight on the lower ski. Transfer the weight to the upper ski, but keep the lower one on the ground. Don't overdo it unless you want to sit down. Tool around for a bit. Try to keep the skis moving forward with no side slipping

2) Try it on a steeper slope where you can use the edges with some angulation. You will of course be edging with the *outside* edge of the upper ski. You will be climbing up the slope with steps of about 6" each time.

When you are bored with this, get going on a fast traverse, angulating over the lower ski, take a step up onto your uphill ski, and as you do so, project your upper body exactly the same way as you have done before, up and forwards towards the fall line, keeping your weight on the uphill ski. As the skis come round to the fall line the uphill ski becomes the downhill ski, and changes from one edge to the other. As soon as the ski has changed from one edge to the other you begin to apply pressure on the front of it with angulation.

The step up accelerates you into the turn by reducing any braking side slip on the lower ski at the start of the turn (see 'contre virage'). It is used significantly by giant slalom racers to gain height on a course, and a variation is used by slalom skiers for the same purpose. You too can use it to gain height when you are traversing round a mountain, and you realise you have to climb as well as going forwards, to reach that restaurant for lunch.

You will notice that stopping after doing several of these high speed turns is an art in itself. It is safer to convert to a few short turns, which applies the brakes slowly, before coming to a stop. Going straight into a standard christie stop from 40 mph with your head and shoulders almost touching the ground, and a fountain of snow spraying skywards, is asking for trouble.

THE POWER TURN

This is the most exciting turn you can make and in racing is really only seen in super GS and downhill. If you have been going fast enough doing the previous turn then you may well have got a feel of it. Again you need a well prepared wide blue to red piste with nobody on it, and preferably no trees on either side. You should have a clear view for at least two hundred metres.

The main difference between this and the previous turn is that you are probably going ten to fifteen mph faster, between fifty and sixty miles an hour. To get going this fast on a traverse you will need to be in the tuck most of the time. Your weight should be well centered between the two skis but as you approach the turn you will need to move onto the uphill ski. In the tuck position and at speed this could really start to hurt those thigh muscles. You should only rise up enough to start the uphill ski turning before you lower into the tuck once more as you cross the fall line. You will be projecting your weight forward and downhill towards the inside of the turn and as you come round you will feel the power coming on. It stands to reason that the skis are on their edges all the way through the turn (apart from the edge change), but there is a *minimum* of reverse camber to provide the long radius arc for a very fast turn. When you get it right it feels like you are being flung round in a bucket on the end of a rope. Well that's what I *imagine* it feels like never having been flung round in a bucket.

With practice it is possible to just make the edge change without *rising up* to unweight the skis at all. By projecting your upper body forward and down the hill, this should provide enough to bring them round. Obviously if you don't come up you will maintain your aerodynamic position in the tuck and not lose speed.

If you start getting into trouble come up out of the tuck and use the natural air brake of your upper body. Your speed will be controlled even more if you are wearing a baggy anorak.

A word of warning! Making these turns should be done in a controlled situation and never willy nilly on a piste with other people skiing at slower speeds in front of you.

CONTRE VIRAGE - TAIL SLIDE

Contre Virage (literally from the French 'against the turn') is a good one for the bar at the day's end, but is a simple enough manoeuvre. All it involves is bringing your downhill hand up and towards your chest in a short arc. If you are going fast enough the back of the skis will slide round. This can have a useful braking effect as the skis are coming round against the fall line, and with angulation can have quite a dramatic result. You can also use it to initiate an edge set prior to breaking into your short turns at the end of those long fast turns we have just described.

How does it work? Once again it's your natural torsion at work again. When you bring your arm up, your shoulder twists round a bit, followed by the muscles down your side, your thigh, your lower leg, your heel, and low and behold the tail of your ski. You may remember that you can achieve the same kind of tail slide by the rapid drop of your upper body in the short turns. The result is the same, but they are different methods for different turns. Contre Virage depends on *steering* while the rapid drop depends on *unweighting*. (back to 'lateral projection')

SHORT TURN WITH LATERAL PROJECTION

This manoeuvre is restricted to skiing slalom gates, but hopefully you are going to practise through gates whenever you can, aren't you?

Lateral projection in a slalom course is used to gain height as well as to accelerate. It is made immediately after the edge set on the lower ski, and is no more than a transfer of weight onto the uphill ski before it comes round into the fall line. It would not seem that a lot of height is gained, but on a steep slope the transfer from lower to upper ski can have a considerable effect if a racer is low in the gate (when combined with avalment), and in theory is more efficient. As we have seen on the long fast turns, if the weight stays on the uphill ski which then becomes the outside weighted ski in the turn, the edge change is going from one edge of this ski to the other. This makes for a smoother transition than from the edge of one ski to the edge of another.

Finally, to round off this chapter, we can couple this lateral projection with avalment, which allows the uphill ski to accelerate into the turn This involves the jet turn technique I mention below. The turn then becomes a short (step) jet turn with lateral projection and avalment. Interesting if a little complicated, huh?

WEDEL TURNS

These turns do not get my vote for practicality, and should not be confused with the short swing turns we have discussed already. These are linked turns made on the flat of the skis, with little edging and no unweighting. They defy the normal rules of unweighting and steering, and rely instead on a waggle of the bottom, minimal knee angulation back and to across the fall line, and a slight push on the downhill heel at the end of the turn. The upper body stays directly over the skis facing forwards, and the skis pivot on the middle of the feet. Wedelling is often used to make nice looking tracks in a few centimetres of fresh snow, and looks quite impressive in front of your friends at the bottom of a run, but it is not going to get you out of trouble on ice, or the steep, or in deep powder. I once skied with a chap who could wedel so fast that his legs and backside were a complete blur. He walked a bit the same way. Do you remember the Twist from the 60's? Wedelling is a bit like the Twist on skis.

JET TURNS

The jet turn is sometimes used by slalom racers to get out of trouble, as well as to accelerate, and is often used by people experimenting in the bumps.

At the moment of the edge set on a short swing turn, try sitting down quickly with the weight on your heels. The maximum you need to sit should have your thighs and legs at about 90o. This is the 'avalment' the bumps were doing for you. Now you are having to do it yourself on to the back of the skis. Having tried it, you will probably fall over unless you can pull back up.

On a steep slalom course, when a racer gets too low in the gates, he may try a jet turn and virtually throw his upper body sideways down the hill at the same time. This means that the skis have a lot of catching up to do as they are describing a wider arc round the gate than his upper body. Hence he accelerates the skis so that they will catch up. Jet turns are fun with a bit of air off the top of a bump, but more often than not are brought off unintentionally as the skis accelerate on the downside.

8 – AVALANCHES & SNOWCRAFT

While skiing with my sister Blanche in the Alps last summer,
I saw a dreadful avalanche about to overcome her.
And as it swept her down the slope I vaguely wondered whether
It would be wise to cut the rope that bound us both together.
I must confess I'm glad I did.........but still I miss the child - poor kid.

Ruthless Rhymes for Heartless Homes - Harry Graham (1874 - 1936)

AVALANCHES

If you can channel all the *fear* you feel for skiing into a phobia for avalanches, then you will have achieved two jobs in one. You will be able to concentrate on the job in hand, yet have a healthy respect for the terrain you are moving over. What has this to do with better skiing? Well, if you can understand a bit about avalanches, you will also learn a little more about the stuff you ski on and the mountains in general, and how to deal with different conditions.

Even the people who study them are still foxed by avalanches and occasionally killed by them; to forecast avalanches can sometimes be like forecasting the weather. There are just too many computations. If we take the two known extremes, there are some conditions that *may be safe*, and others that will *certainly be dangerous*.

SIMON DEWHURST

Cold fresh snow consists of beautiful little crystals with sharp edges and points that act as hooks. After these pretty little things have touched down they get cosy with each other (but not immediately), and start to interlock under the influence of gravity – unlike humans, who rely on gluwein and a friendly smile etc.

So this tempting carpet of sparkling angel poop is lying there, all sort of joined up, waiting to be vandalised by the likes of you and me. Let's take this example: sixty centimetres of it has fallen during a cold night on to older well settled snow that is similar in texture to the new fall. The slope gradient averages 25 degrees with a large bump at the top, dropping away quite quickly, and then gradually sloping up towards the bottom. It looks orgasmic. The weather is cold and sunny, and the snow all fluffy when you kick it. Do you go? You bet your backside you do. But will you die? Well, in this situation you could be all right, and I'll explain why shortly.

Now take this second example, and this is the sort of scenario that comes to life yet brings only death, regularly taking out powder freaks every year. It has snowed sixty centimetres again during another cold night, but this time it has fallen onto old snow that has been blown by the wind into a thin smooth crust. The slope is the same, and looks just as good, but do you go? Of course you don't. And why not? Because if you do, you may not be around to finish this little book.

In each example the fresh snow looks exactly the same on top, but why is the second one so dangerous? In the first example all the snowflakes have nestled into each other, *and* into the older snow beneath, but in the second case the new snow has *not* locked into the old. Also, in both cases, there is a point on top of the bump where the snow is under tension. The convex shape of the bump tends to stretch the snow crystals apart.

Lower down as the gradient slopes upwards, the snow is not under tension, and this concave shape tends to prevent the crystals from separating. In the first case a skier can cut the snow under tension, and some of it may come away, but because it is tied into the old snow underneath, it may hold. In the second example, however, there is no interlocking with the old snow, so when skis cut a swathe through the new stuff, especially where it is under tension on the bump, CRUMPH, and the lot goes, thundering down on the slippery base. As it comes to a stop near the bottom it builds up quite a pressure, and anyone who has been unfortunate enough to be carried down and buried underneath it, can be locked solid, unable to move even a finger. This kind of avalanche may not necessarily go just when or where it has been cut. It may wait until you are half way down and having a smoke break (although I hope you don't smoke). Even noise and vibration can set it off. And it doesn't need to be sixty centimetres deep. Sixty centimetres is about twenty inches; even *four* inches spread over a wide area can be lethal.

I have only mentioned a simple slab avalanche that kills regularly, but there are many more kinds that do the job just as well.

Both stable and unstable snow conditions depend on many factors, including weather conditions, altitude, surface structure, gradient, and depth of snowfalls. Wherever you ski, you can think about these things. How much snow is underneath you and how is the surface made up? Are you high up skiing over rocky ground above the tree line, or are you on dead grass low down in the meadows? What piste lies in the sun at different times of the day, and what shape will it be in during mid afternoon (a particularly popular time for avalanches late in the season)? Ask yourself these questions, and common sense will make you choose wisely. A steep narrow couloir, concave from side to side on a firm base, could hold, whereas powder snow on a lesser gradient lower down the mountain could go. Avalanches are like mushrooms; *if you're not sure, don't touch them.*

This is not really the book to start a technical dissertation on avalanches, but think about everything mentioned here, and you will get a feel for the stuff you are skiing on, a feel for the lie of the land, a feel for what lies under the snow. You will start to enjoy the mountains more. This is why I have lumped avalanches with snowcraft. One slides into the other - so to speak. If you can assess the snow type, temperature, and surface structure, you will be more aware of what you are skiing on, why it feels like it does, and what you should avoid.

Let me finish with a story about an avalanche. This was some time ago in 1973. Two men were skiing off piste in Geilo Norway in early March. The temperature was below freezing, perhaps minus 5 Celsius, the sun was shining and eight inches of fresh snow had fallen two nights before. They were walking under a six foot cornice over which some of the powder snow had been blown and settled into a small back bowl. The back bowl was no wider than a couple of hundred yards with a three hundred yard slope before it bottomed out into some birch trees, but for Geilo Norway it was something out of the ordinary and something special.

The man in front continued walking under the cornice while his friend, who was about three yards behind decided he couldn't wait any longer and started off. After three turns he stopped and the hairs on the back of his neck stood up. He knew there was something wrong with the snow although he couldn't say what it was. It may have been that most of it was blown snow although it was reasonably light, or it may have been a hard snow base he could feel underneath. Of course it could just have been his sixth sense. Whatever it was made him stop and turn to his friend, Benni, who had now moved a few more yards under the cornice.

If it's possible to shout 'Benni' quietly that's what he did. He then put his finger to his lips, and stuck his hand up in a sign to stop. Benni stopped. The skier took his skis off and treading as carefully as possible began to walk straight back up the hill. It was only about fifteen yards. At the very moment he reached the path under the cornice, there was a thud and the ground shook. It seemed as if the whole mountain was moving. A huge crack fifty yards long opened up just below their feet. The depth of the slab that had broken off was only eight inches deep yet it made a noise like a stampede of water buffalo. Within about five seconds the thundering stopped as the front end of the avalanche hit the upturn and the birch trees.

We both skied down on the firm base (I expect you've guessed that I was Benni's friend), and gaped at the six foot wall of snow that had piled up. It was set hard with great chunks of solid snow the size of suitcases welded into each other. We were very lucky; if we had been buried by this monster it would have already crushed the life out of us. If we had just been caught by an arm or a leg, it would have needed a spade to dig us out. If just our heads had been caught we would already have been suffocated.

This was a lesson early on in my skiing career that I have never forgotten. Of course there have been temptations since; fortunately, because of this early experience, I've been able to check myself or the people around me. It *is* tempting to go off into the great white yonder, but once again don't be tempted to try anything you're not sure of. Most of the locals, who are keen skiers, will quite happily tell you whether the conditions in such and such a place are all right, or whether they should be avoided like the plague. I'm not being a spoilsport because nine times out of ten with care you *will* be all right, but carry awareness and caution with you all the time.

SNOWCRAFT

Snowcraft to me means using the soles of your feet as well as the old grey matter to work for you. Next time you are standing still at the bottom of a lift, waiting for George, who has forgotten his ski pass, run your skis backwards and forwards on the snow. Do you see that solid little lump of snow the size of a pomegranate near the tips? Run one ski over it. Can you feel it? Just imagine how sensitive your foot must be. Even with your eyes closed you may be able to guess what it is. The signal, 'I am a pomegranate sized lump of snow', is travelling two feet back along the ski, half an inch through it, up through another half inch of boot, through a nice fresh sock, and into the sole of your foot, and you can still feel it. Wow! Now that George has turned up, go for a run, and start to FEEL where you are going. Move very slowly over an easy, empty piste and close your eyes for a moment. What can you feel through the soles of your feet?

You can extend this new found sensitivity further, and start gauging where to find the best snow, the worst ice, good grass skiing, etc. For example, following the sun does not necessarily give you the best snow conditions. Remember that during the day, the sun may warm up a southern facing slope, and provide nice spring snow, but from the start to the end of the day the conditions can vary from boiler plate ice through to slush. You can reckon this out from the time of year, the altitude, and the lie of the land.

Take another example. If you are skiing off piste, and the snow feels really heavy, you will learn that all may not be lost. The heavy snow might have had the sun on it for only half an hour, and gone cruddy, but the stuff just over the ridge, and still in slight shade, could be magic. If the slope is at a very high altitude, say at over 9,000 ft in the European Alps, the sun may never soften the snow up until late in the season, and it could lie powdery for days between snow falls. Snow on a north facing slope can be the best in a resort at any altitude, and although you may find your face getting cold, you often have the mountain to yourself. A sunny slope obviously attracts everyone, but it is hardly conducive to better skiing when all your concentration is channelled into avoiding that enormously fat woman careering across your path in the lilac shell suit. Okay, so you're only out for a week, and there's no point in going back to the Big Smoke (London) looking PALE, so why not spend an hour or so before the sun strengthens practising on a nice empty slope with good snow on it. There are such places.

Remember about mileage; once you have warmed up, ski hard and push yourself a bit, then slow down and concentrate on the snowcraft thing for a while. As the terrain changes from steep to gradual and back again, and the snow changes from yielding to icy and maybe to slush, feel what is happening to your weight, your balance, and how the snow is sliding under the skis. Try different turns. On steep bits try to see how many short linked turns you can do in a given distance. On gradual open pistes go for the long, fast, and smooth variety. When you get to bumps slow down, and using the bumps to unweight the skis, see how slowly you can go without stopping. This is a great exercise in the bumps and quite difficult! Notice that you speed up over the hard or icy steep side of a bump, and come to a sudden stop in all that loose stuff in the trough before the next one. You will have to combine running forward with some pretty fancy side slipping to keep up a constant slow speed.

If there is some fresh snow around next to the piste, have a go on that too, but remember that you are going to have to make radical alterations to your technique (see 'Off Piste'). Remember too that you will have to alter your technique often, even on different pisted conditions. If you can accept this at an early stage, you will realise that certain conditions are impossible for you to ski on. Be resigned about this and you will avoid a lot of frustration and depression. White outs, cloying slush, and boiler plate icy bumps are the worst conditions you will find on the piste, and will test your talents for survival to their limits. Simply regarding these conditions as a little local difficulty will keep you sane. A good lunch close to the cable car station or some other form of mountain transport to get you home is the best substitute.

9A – GOODBYE TO THE BAD STUFF

You will only be able to overcome your limitations and other negative influences if you are fully aware of them, and are prepared to take the right action. This may seem quite obvious, but do you know what if anything (besides your technical ability) is holding back your progress? Fear, of course, comes immediately to mind, and maybe even badly fitting ski boots, but suppose I say 'ski school', or even 'holiday', would you be surprised?

Many of these negative influences become positive ones if you can sort them out and work on them, and you will find that there is interaction between many of them.

FEAR, FITNESS AND FALLING

'I have been seriously afraid at times but I have used my fear as a stimulating factor rather than allowing it to paralyse me' Sir Edmund Hillary – 'View from the Summit' 1999

I have not cobbled together this sub-title for its alliterative quality, but rather to demonstrate that these three elements are all interlinked, and that their negative aspects are the three most important influences to affect better skiing. If you can sort them out and act on them, you will have just about cracked it. Is it really that easy to attain nirvana and enlightenment?

Fear is the most common handicap against better skiing. After thirty years of teaching skiing I have not found an easy solution, and I don't believe there is one.

Do not confuse fear with nervous excitement. Nervous excitement produces adrenaline and the will to go. Once you are going, you become relaxed and businesslike, and everything is ticketyboo. Fear in its worst form is a state of mental and physical paralysis, an inability to budge, the muscles in a contracted state of immobility, as you agonise over the mogul field ahead, or the cat, or the milk bill, etc. Now if you go sliding off down the piste in this state, the things that you hope won't happen almost certainly will.

LOSS OF NERVE

Let's start by dividing fear into two separate states. Decide first of all whether it is due to lack of confidence, or loss of nerve. These are rather nebulous phrases to describe similar emotions. You may be able to do something about lack of confidence, but loss of nerve can be irreversible.

Quite often people who have mastered a particular sport eventually lose their nerve. They realise that they can no longer cope with the mental and physical pressures, and will often make the right decision to hang up their boots, or put away their fishing rod. Those who continue often subject themselves to a life of misery, and a ski holiday is not supposed to be like that!

There are also people who try to ski with pathological afflictions like vertigo and agoraphobia. (I truly have had people with these phobias to teach!) For them I have never been able to offer suitable advice. These problems should be confronted by somebody more qualified than myself

There are also many people who have lost their nerve for other reasons. Having children can often lower women's fear thresholds to the extent that although they are prepared to enjoy easy skiing, they have no more interest in anything that is physically challenging (and I don't include raising children).

There are others who have perhaps had a bad fall or even a car accident, and the physical damage and pain, even after recovery, may have affected them psychologically as well. Loss of nerve through accident and injury can be reversed to some extent, and as long as a skier can accept his psychological limitations, he can still enjoy pottering down the easy slopes. Often after a really bad accident a skier will return to do even better, this being especially true with racers, and has a lot to do with pain thresholds, fitness, and other things that I discuss later.

If you finally make the decision that alpine skiing is not for you, I will tell you here that you have made the right decision! It is a rough, tough sport and if you want to be good at it, dithering in hope will get you nowhere.

Perhaps I should say a quick word about cross country skiing here as many people have found it a more acceptable form of skiing for their make up. It has many of the attractions of downhill skiing without the hassles. Practically every alpine resort has paths laid out through the woods and round the lakes. You can actually say 'Good Morning' to people, and stop and talk about absolutely nothing to complete strangers if you want. It can be a very gentle, friendly form of exercise, and quite therapeutic, and it takes very little time to learn. Most ski schools have instructors who are well qualified, and quite often after a hard working season of teaching, I have gone cross country skiing to wind down, and to welcome the Spring.

SIMON DEWHURST

For any cross country skiers reading this who object to my remarks about it being a gentle form of exercise just let me repeat that it *can* be gentle. At competitive level I would put it on a par with rowing in an eight. It is hell while you're doing it and wonderful when it's over.

LACK OF CONFIDENCE

If there is not much we can do about loss of nerve, there is lots to do about lack of confidence. Sometimes lack of confidence leads to a loss of nerve, but this should be avoided at all costs! Do you physically feel on some days that you cannot go down a particular slope, but that on other days you can? Nevertheless, off you go in the hope that something may come together. The skis are flapping around a lot, you are sitting back, and the weather looks bleak. You may even have a bit of a hangover after that amazing party last night, and you have finished all the Resolve. Suddenly you hit some ice or a bump, and omygod! The minimal amount of confidence or 'go' that you had earlier completely disintegrates. It is a physical state rather than a mental one, and can be quite often the result of tiredness, or any other biological malfunction. Whatever the reason, your physical state affects you mentally to the extent that you develop a feeling of inadequacy. You have two choices; you can either pack up and go home for the day, which is the sensible decision, or else you can blunder on until you frighten yourself and possibly lose your nerve.

Never despair if you find you cannot ski on some days. Stop and give up. I know you are only out on a six day break, but even the best skiers have their off days. They usually pack up and go home to read a good book. Whatever you choose to do, don't struggle on in the hope that you may recover. You *may* recover, but more often than not you won't, and you could easily do the sort of confidence-losing damage we are trying to avoid. In short, be aware of your limitations.

FALLING

It is a tricky one to draw the line between where a fall stops being a fall, and becomes a crash. By the time you start thinking about how to react in a crash, you are actually airborne. You *can* do something, however, and that is relax as you go. When I say relax, I really mean Reeeelax with a capital R. This also applies to lesser falls as well of course. If you Reeeelax, it is surprising how little damage you will do even after the most spectacular wipe out.

You must forget the 'How-did-you-do-today?-Wow-I-didn't-fall-once' syndrome. If you are going to become a better skier by pushing yourself, you can't avoid falling. You don't reckon Alberto Tomba or Franz Klammer got where they did without a few crashes do you? Anyway, you are reading the words of the world's greatest authority on crashes, and I'm still alive. (See Ch1A - Release Bindings)

There is something else to remember about falling which may help you to reduce fear. Within reason you will find that the steeper a slope goes, the less you will hurt yourself as you hit the ground. I'm not suggesting that you should experiment by taking the Devil's Couloir straight, but normally the falls that hurt the most are the ones on the flat. This has to do with relative mass and gravity. You will slide a lot on a steep slope, and gradually come to a stop, whereas on a flat path, for example, you will go Splat, and be all of a jumble on the deck.

Now it follows that if you are going to fall a lot, you are also going to injure yourself a few times. Injuries can be anything from a sprained thumb to a broken neck, with pulled knee ligaments (being the most common) somewhere in between. It may surprise you that a survey of ski accidents, made by a French medical insurance company, showed that under 7% of reported injuries in the French Alps during the season were broken legs, and that only 0.3% of all skiers sustained a reported injury. So when people say that they are afraid of skiing in case they break a leg, we can see that their chances of doing so are about 5000 to 1 against. These figures assume, of course, that you don't *try* to break your leg, or other equally important bits, by cranking up your bindings as tight as they will go, leaping off a cliff that turns out to be higher than you expected, or running headlong into a ski lift pylon. These can make for entertaining skiing, but they severely increase the chances of injury.

We can deduce, therefore, that serious injuries are few and far between, but you must accept that skiing is a contact sport. Hopefully, unlike the various games of football, most of the contact will be with the ground, but it *can* be rough and tough; if you have been brought up on these sort of games you will understand and accept that injury is inevitable, and must be acceptable in skiing. It is quite difficult to accept this fact with the apparent paradox that skiing is a sort of gentle relaxation therapy. Any hard physical exercise tends to be mentally relaxing, but contact sports were never intended to be soft on the body. Alpine skiing was invented in the nineteen twenties by sturdy university students flogging themselves up and down three thousand vertical metres of mountain a day through deep snow. They didn't particularly mind about hurting themselves, and they must have been remarkably fit, but they were, remember, the first *holiday* skiers.

Fitness plays a crucial part. It not only enables you to ski properly, but also prevents injury and reduces fear. If you are fit, your muscles and your mind will react faster, your ligaments and joints will be more supple, and you will feel good. If you are unfit, you are starting out with a ball and chain round your neck and your head in a paper bag. You won't be able to do the job properly, and may very soon start to lose confidence and feel frightened. I have discussed fitness as a positive aspect earlier, but I really believe that unfitness is one of the main causes of fear, so if you want to be a better skier, dust off the old trainers and get going. Getting fit involves a certain amount of pain, and you begin to realise that your body is capable of going through contortions that you didn't think possible. When you get on skis, your body will be able to cope with the wrenching and battering that much more easily. If you can get your pre-skiing exercises right, it is quite possible to ski all of the first day without any ill effects at all, but as with most things in this cruel world of ours, you must put in a lot of effort beforehand.

BAD EQUIPMENT

'A bad workman always blames his tools' goes the saying, but I have always found that a bad workman, cack-handed though he may be, doesn't really know whether his tools are up to the job or not. Quite often the tools are making him do a bad job in the first place, rather than the other way round. If your boots are loose at the heel, you can angulate as much as you like, but the initial movement of your feet will not be transmitted through the boot to put the skis on edge. If the edges of the skis are blunt and pitted, the skis will not grip in the turns, and perhaps won't even slide properly. You may be right in thinking that a few holes drilled in the bottom of each ski would slow you down nicely and thank the Lord for small mercies, but have you ever tried to ski with a great gouge in one ski? It feels like there is something nasty stuck to the bottom of your shoe, and you can't get it off. It is vital to know how your kit works, and what to do to maintain it.

SIMON DEWHURST

9B – GOODBYE TO THE BAD STUFF

SKI SCHOOL

Is this right? Isn't ski school supposed to teach us how to ski? How can it be a negative influence?

It is quite true that with skiing there must be some sort of a teaching process, but there can often be a lot wrong with ski school. A system that initially sets out to help and encourage, can actually handicap those who want to use it.

Now of course I am generalising, and let me say, before I am shafted on the end of a ski pole, that I have come across many superb teachers, whose methods are a credit to the system, if only the system was not bogged down with so much technical emphasis, and an unassailable belief in its own importance. The ski school has unconsciously adopted the light bulb syndrome. Invent a perfect light bulb and the manufacturers would soon be out of business. Invent an efficient instruction system, and most novices would only need a week at the most, with an occasional coaching session for a morning each holiday. Instead what often happens is that a pupil is bombarded with an appalling mixture of conflicting instructions delivered by different teachers, who don't speak the same language as their class. Perfectly executed movements are demonstrated by an immaculate, yet inarticulate, bronzed Adonis, who is really only in the resort to notch a few up on his belt. It is hardly surprising that I meet skiers who have been in and out of the ski school all their lives like hardened recidivist cat burglars going in and out of prison.

The ski school must exist, and its main purpose should be to show its pupils *how* to learn. The learning process itself should then be developed by the pupil on his own, clocking up the miles, and presenting himself with attainable challenges. Of course the ski school is also there to provide other services such as guiding and kindergartens, but it is the very teaching methods that concern me here. If you find as a pupil that you do not understand an instruction, or find it impossible to carry out, and cannot get the teacher to show you how, then you must question yourself: 'Is this doing any good? Am I any wiser? Am I wasting money? Should I not go and buy a copy of 'Secrets of Better Skiing?'

It is easy for me to say 'caveat emptor', but how can a buyer beware if he is ignorant of the pitfalls? A beginner is going to find this practically impossible, but it will be a lot easier for beginners and better skiers alike if they can find a good instructor. There is wisdom in looking for impartial advice from someone who can tell you where to find the best instructor, or the best ski school, or even the best resort for what you want.

I have thought for some time that ski instruction should include theoretical considerations, which could be discussed at the end of a hard day's skiing in a cosy little hut at the bottom of the mountain with a large mug of gluwein! The instructor produces a boot and a ski and actually tells you what they are about and how they work. Perhaps he even tells you about different kinds of snow, how to avoid avalanches, other skiers, and everything else that cannot be readily discussed out on the mountainside. For every pupil this would be part of any weekly ski course, and would give them an idea of their surroundings and the stuff they were skiing on.

PUTTING A BEGINNER ON THE RIGHT TRACK

I have often heard people trying to teach their friends and wives and relations to ski without any idea what they were talking about. I certainly didn't. It was always pretty obvious that the pupil didn't either, and I wonder how many of these pupils went on to become skiers or whether they just gave up.

Sometimes out of frustration for the system, or because romance may be in the air, you, the better skier, will have the urge to teach a beginner yourself. Now I am not recommending this as *always* being the best way, but I can hardly say don't do it. After all, by the time you have read this little tome, you *will* be an expert won't you? It is as well to run through a few basic rules if you are going to teach someone to ski or just going to give them some advice.

Remember that a beginner will invariably be in a state similar to shock. He will be able to take very little in by way of technical guff, and everything will have to be shown by demonstration. Even the act of putting his boots and skis on will be difficult.

Keep your vocabulary to a minimum and keep it simple. Work out simple key words to show how it should be done. Always encourage. Always say: 'Do it this way'. *Never* say: *'Don't* do this'. *'Don't* do that.' It is too confusing.

In short, **always make positive statements.** If necessary point out a fault by demonstration with a careful explanation of what the pupil is doing wrong, followed by the correct method. Do repeat movements and exaggerate them if necessary. Be patient. Make exercises simple for the pupil and increase his challenges gradually. Be sensitive to his needs, and think long and hard about the way you are going to explain something before you start to explain it. Try to remember how it was for you when you were a beginner, and say it how *you* would like it to have been said. Finally, if you don't like teaching or don't think you can do it, don't teach!

You may just be wondering why this book is turning into a ski instructors' manual, but unless you are going to resist the irresistible by imparting your own knowledge to somebody else, then you may as well be aware of the pitfalls. Going back to what I said at the beginning of this section, I have heard instructions from amateur teachers that a rubber-limbed orang-utan would find difficult to do. Things like 'Bend the lower shoulder towards the back of the ski', 'Point the upper ski downhill' and 'Lean back!' could severely impair a beginner's progress.

If you can understand why these instructions will not really work, then perhaps you may make a teacher! Working out how you would explain a movement to somebody else is no bad thing at all, as it can help *you* to understand what *you* are doing, and get you to think while you are doing it! Beware, however, of doing it at a friend's expense.

HOLIDAYS, MONEY AND MOTIVATION

The length of your holiday must affect your progress, and the more you ski the better you should be. As most people only ski for a week nowadays, there is never a great deal of time to get into your stride. It really boils down to how you rate skiing; the best skiers on the mountain, apart from the natives, are the ones who do it for one or two months a winter. They are either rich and can afford the time, or else they have thrown everything into skiing, and discarded everything else except the old two-tone VW camper.

It is possible, however, that if you are highly motivated, you can be in tip top ski condition the minute you step into your skis, and it may only take an hour or so to get the feel back. To do this you will have had to spend at least a couple of months working out with your own exercise programme, but it is possible!

Of course there are priorities on a ski holiday; if the main priority for a particular person is comfort, followed by good food, relaxation, and skiing, in that order, it stands to reason that if he were to put *skiing* on top of the list, followed by relaxation, good food, and comfort, then his motivation would be that much stronger. His money would last longer too, and he could spend longer skiing. This all sounds a bit simplistic, but if you are really keen, you will overcome little problems like lack of time and money. Whacking another week on your holiday, staying at a cheaper hotel or in a friend's apartment, and organising the holiday yourself, should save you a bundle. Telephone your boss towards the end of week one, with a feeble excuse about an obscure mountain virus, or avalanches blocking the approach roads.

CORRECTING FAULTS

This is something that I have left till last. Every other ski book I have come across seems to treat this particular subject with a lot more consideration than I can bring myself to contemplate. By the time you have read this far, and if you have managed to avoid suffering from a brain seizure or total overload, then it seems to me that you will know how to correct any faults that may arise off your own bat. It also contradicts my philosophy of never saying 'No! *Don't* do that!' when I should be saying 'Do *this*', meaning to a great extent that if you do '*this*' you will avoid doing '*that*'! Understood?

However, in order to make sure that you do understand perfectly what I have touched on already I may as well mention a few things again. Basically we're just looking at the same issues from a different angle.

Upper Body Position

Let's start with the upper body position when doing short turns. We've seen that if your upper body swings in towards the mountain at the wrong time the skis are quite likely to swing round after it and you may accidentally start coming down the mountain backwards. It is unlikely that you do want to do this as you won't be able to see where you are going and could quite easily run into someone. The reason for doing it is what we should really tackle. If this doesn't exist, neither will the problem. It seems to me that a *misplaced* desire for self survival may be the reason for turning inwards. Often the downhill shoulder comes up too in an 'Oh no you're not going to get me' sort of attitude. The mountain *will* get you if you turn your body into the hill! So mantra number one is **Face down the hill doing short turns.**

Weight Transfer

As your technique speeds up, and you start to do short linked turns at the speed of light, the instruction 'apply weight to outside ski' sometimes gets given by your brain half a second too late as you start the turn. The uphill ski, instead of turning all the way, rides over the downhill one, which has also started to turn but not as much. By this time the instruction 'apply weight to the outside ski' has been received loud and clear by your lower leg but it's too late. You are now well into the fall line with skis crossed, not knowing whether you are Arthur or Martha.

As we have discussed elsewhere it is quite possible for you to turn on the uphill ski, but you need to implant the instruction 'weight downhill ski' into your brain until it becomes a reflex action first, and believe me it can take a long time when you are not thinking about it! I crossed my skis a hundred times back in the seventies when Parablacks were fashionable. These were four inch high plastic bridges that fitted onto the top of the skis at the front; as the upper ski tried to cross the lower one it was stopped momentarily by a Parablack, and hopefully gave enough time to avoid the problem. They worked well and I have seen them around occasionally nowadays, so if crossing your skis is a problem, stick some on. But at the same time remember the second mantra and say it whenever you need to at every turn '**weight the downhill ski**', or if that's too much to say every time just '**left ski' 'right ski' 'left ski' 'right ski'**, meaning of course 'transfer weight'.

Sitting Back

This mostly happens on ice because of fear, in the bumps because of computer malfunction, and in powder snow because someone has told you to do it. I can understand the fear on ice but remember that the skis won't work unless your weight is in the right place, and on ice this is *especially* true. If you sit back very little of the ski edge will be cutting into the ice, but with your weight over the middle of the ski, or even slightly forward, then you will have the control you badly need. You must make a positive decision, ie: this is ice and I must keep my weight forward - say it out loud if necessary - *'Ice! Keep weight forward!'*

The easiest way out of this is to apply the driving analogy ie: keep your hands in the bottom of your line of vision at all times until you have got it right, as though holding the steering wheel of a car in the short turns, or, if you are doing long fast turns, as though you are holding the handlebars of a motorbike with your *uphill* shoulder very slightly higher than your *lower* shoulder as you come round in the turn.

SIMON DEWHURST

10 – DIVERSIONS

SPEED SKIING

Does 60 or 70 mph sound a little slow? How about doubling that to 130 mph or faster? All you need to do is get yourself a pair of 240 cm skis, get an FIS licence and whoooosh ...

Organised speed skiing began in the late fifties up on the Monte Rosa glacier bordering Italy and Switzerland. Here at 12000ft in the thin air under the Matterhorn, brave men hurled themselves straight down the side of a glacier without turning. The maximum gradient was about 62 degrees. I say 'about' as the glacier kept moving and each year was a slightly different shape. By 1970 the 200kph (120 mph) benchmark had been passed, and has been climbing ever since. The problem with the Cervinia course was that it had two crevasses on it near the top which the skiers had to jump over before they really started motoring, and the outrun at the bottom went up so suddenly that the compression was like carrying two bags of cement in each pocket. When the cracks got too big in the late seventies, it was time to change the venue to Les Arcs in France which for many years was the fastest course in the world. The world record is now held by Ivan Origone from Italy, who skied down a course in Vars, France in March 2016. His speed was 158.42mph which is about forty miles an hour faster than a free falling skydiver.

During the eighties the sport was opened up to allow all comers, rather than just renegade downhillers sponsored by their national federations. Courses can be set up anywhere suitable as long as they are off piste, and high speeds can be reached on gradients of no more than 45 degrees. The qualifications needed to take part are bottle and some skiing ability. Technically you have to be able to get into a very low tuck, hold it even when a 100 mph wind is trying to rip you apart, and come to a safe snow plough stop on 8 ft long skis. You also need to be fit.

Speed skiing is a relatively safe sport, and thankfully is now well controlled in competition. Runs are begun from low down on the hill through 100 metre traps at low speeds. Eliminations are made on the way up, and those who lack the necessary stability are also weeded out. The most common injuries are friction burns from the snow, and the occasional knee injury as the safety bindings need to be well cranked up to cope with the vibration. A fall at 100 mph usually releases the skis, but the friction between the snow and the thin rubber regulation suits tends to melt them rather quickly. People of all ages take part. The oldest of them all, Kalevi Haakinen, tried to reach the 200 kph mark for twenty years, and eventually made it aged 60.

It is cheap to take part if you can borrow a pair of skis and a suit, and the local alpine ski club wherever you happen to be will usually sponsor you for a small joining fee. The expense comes when you want to commute from your own country to various events. Regardless of the expense, it is the easiest way to take part in proper competition. There is a lot of hanging about in the sunshine, listening to bad jokes, but the buzz as the skis leave the ground at 100 mph is something to remember.

SIMON DEWHURST

FREESTYLE - BASIC BALLET EXERCISES

Freestyle skiing has come a long way since the swinging sixties and now comprises some serious competitive disciplines. One that is missing now is ballet or dancing to music on skis. This type of ballet should not be confused with Swan Lake. Watching people twirling around on one ski while the other one is up behind their head, may not be your cup of tea, but some of these manoeuvres which I have put together as a basic exercise programme, will help your balance enormously, and provide you and your friends with hours of endless fun - rather like a whoopee cushion. Not only that, they get your brain to think about where they are at any given time in space; they do wonders for your spatial awareness.

I have listed the movements starting with the easiest, and there is to some extent a natural progression that will help you through to the finish. You don't have to go out and do them all on the same day though. Choose the easiest flat slope you can find away from people. You are going to fall a lot!

1 360 degrees on two skis: Just go ahead and try it with little direction from me. Keep the skis parallel, and dig a pole into the snow like using an oar as a brake to start you off if necessary. Think about the weight transfer. When does it change from one ski to the other? When you are going backwards think about a backwards snow plough to get back round.

2 Forward crossover: Stand on a traverse and lift the downhill ski up in front of you, and put it down on the uphill side of the other one. With your weight on it, lean forward and lift the other one up behind you, putting it down uphill of the first one. Do it a few times until you get the hang of it, and then do it on the move. Next try it on the other traverse. Bottom ski over the top ski, top ski round behind, and back.

3 Royal Christie: This is excellent practice for feeling the weight on your uphill ski. Move off on a traverse. Lift up the downhill ski. You can just lift it off the ground to start with (later you can put it round behind you up in the air). Now try and turn *up* into the hill on the uphill ski. Move your weight forward a little. Use a pole prodded into the snow to get you started. Anything can happen. As soon as you start going backwards or stop put the other ski down. That was half of a Royal Christie; now for the full one.

Moving on the same traverse, lift the *uphill* ski in the air, and turn downhill and across the fall line on the downhill ski. This is quite tricky as your brain will probably refuse to accept the instruction. It is know as prejudice.

Now try both exercises again on the other traverse.

Try linking the turns without stopping, and eventually try to get the free ski up behind your back with your free leg nice and straight. You will need to lean quite far forward. Hold your hands and your poles out to the side for balance, and if you lead with you outside shoulder and arm in front of the other one, this will help your upper body to turn the ski. Above all, look cool.

4 360 degrees on one ski: Turn to your right while you are on the right ski, and to your left while on the left ski. You may need to make a pole prod. Keep the unweighted ski just off the ground.

5 Skiing backwards: Start with a snow plough, and work up to a stem christie. lean forward to prevent the ski tails going into the snow.

6 Backwards 360 on one ski: Move backwards on a traverse. Lift uphill ski. Come round backwards into the fall line on lower ski. Repeat on other traverse. Lean forward.

7 Backwards Royal Christie: If you have got this far, go for it on your own!

If you can only get to the second of these exercises, you will have felt the new experience of moving over the snow on the uphill ski. By completing all of them, you will have stretched ligaments (hopefully not too far), worked unused muscles, and most importantly built resistance for the future against unnecessary crashes. If you are interested in developing this branch of freestyle skiing further, get the details from the back of the book.

JUMPING

The Pre-Jump

Watching ski racing on the television you would be forgiven for thinking that the downhillers are trying to cut their time by doing thirty or forty metre jumps, rather than rattling the whole way down on the ice. In fact a jump usually slows a racer down as it often takes a longer route than the course on the ground, and the landing tends to brake the skis. To ensure that he will be in the air for the shortest time, he needs to take certain precautions. It is often quite adequate to absorb the smaller bumps with avalment, but with rapid changes of gradient on a downhill course, combined with speeds up to 80 mph, this just isn't possible. Instead the racer will resort to a pre-jump.

Just before he gets to the point on the jump that would send him into orbit without remedial action, a racer does the equivalent of a standing jump. With good timing he should be coming down from his standing jump as he passes over the crest. With bad timing he'll be wishing he'd put the cat out. The timing is therefore crucial, and as if he didn't have enough to worry about, there is often the added problem of compression. Imagine that the hill goes into a little dip before rising up to the lip of a jump. Skiing into this at speed could make our intrepid downhiller feel twice his own weight for an instant, and almost at the same time he has to pre-jump. Downhill skiers are remarkably fit, and have good memories.

How does all this affect you? If you are going to do long fast turns on the piste safely, then you need to practise pre-jumping. The hillock you were skiing over before at 30 mph, is going to feel quite different at 50 or 60 mph. It is quite easy trying out a pre-jump over a small bump, perhaps not more than a foot high. Approach it on a traverse in a relaxed upright position. Go down slightly, and as you come up jump, bending the knees and bringing the skis up to you. You should just be off the ground as you go over the crown of the bump, and yet be starting to come down. Extend your legs to absorb the landing. In time it will be as easy as getting out of bed, and more fun as you progress on to larger bumps at faster speeds. In the air you should maintain the take off position with your knees up, and only lower them to absorb the landing. In an ideal world your arms would be down by your side, and ever so slightly forward. This will encourage you to keep the skis tips down and your body ever so slightly forward. As you do not live in an ideal world, remember that your arms and poles can be used like windmills to save you if necessary.

The Jump - going for Air

You can of course force a jump over the smallest bump. Approach the top of the bump in a slight tuck, and as you reach it, push down hard on both legs, standing up as you do so. As you take off, bring your knees up, and then lower them just before landing. Make sure there is no one on the blind landing side of bigger jumps. If you are going on a fun jumping day with some friends, *make sure there is somebody signalling the all clear from the jump itself.* There could be somebody on the landing side all of a jumble, and it is difficult to make course corrections when you are in mid air, and trying to avoid a possible manslaughter charge.

Choose a jump with a steep landing. If you fall you will hurt yourself less on a steep slope than on a flat one. The most dangerous jump is the one that lifts you vertically into the air, and then drops you on to a flat landing. The most satisfying straight jump is the one where you take off and follow the line of the hill for perhaps ten metres never more than half a metre off the snow. You will find that you can start on small bumps, and build up gradually.

Cliffs Rocks and Cornices

A ski instructor was taking his class off piste and had skirted round a huge thirty foot cliff. All the class followed him dutifully, apart from one lone novice who had got left behind. The instructor stopped about fifty metres below the cliff and looked back in horror to see the straggler perched on the cliff edge in obvious confusion. 'Don't jump', the instructor cried 'Come round the side - **it's a precipice!'** *The novice did not seem to hear him and edged even closer. 'No!! Go round the side, it's a precipice!! Oh dear'. The novice had jumped. From where the instructor and his class stood the crash looked appalling. The instructor sidestepped up to the poor fellow who was surrounded by pieces of broken kit, and sitting in the snow looking dazed. 'Why did you do that?' he said 'Didn't you hear* *me telling you it was a precipice?' 'Precipice?'* replied the skier *'I thought you said 'piece of piss''*.

For those unfamiliar with Anglo Saxon colloquialisms this phrase means 'very easy'

You've been looking at that cornice just off the top of the chair lift for a few days now haven't you? It's not very high is it, only about a metre on to a steep landing? So you ski over to it – crumbs. It's higher than you thought. The outrun looks a bit steep too. Trouble is, you've got to do it now. They're all watching. Here goes ..... whoosh .... goodness me, you're still standing.

That's all there is too it really. Start small. Take a good look at the landing. Make sure there are no rocks or other obstacles in the way, and push off, literally. I always aim slightly off to one side on a slight angle, rather than straight, to catch a braking turn early so to speak. If you find you want to do more jumps like this one go for something ever so slightly bigger next time. Solid cornices are good jumps to work on because they usually vary in height along their length, and because more often than not the outrun is quite steep, which prevents landing accidents. Rocks and cliffs should be examined quite carefully from the edge, and if necessary from below as well to check for protruding rocks and trees on the way down. Whatever you do, don't go off something you haven't looked at first!

To avoid embarrassment do not try and jump into Corbett's Couloir for a first try. Practise somewhere secretly if possible and *then* book your two weeks in Jackson Hole.

Food for Thought

We were all taught to put our weight on the downhill ski when we were learning, and even throughout this book most of the instructions emphasise the importance of weighting the downhill ski. But *why* do we weight the downhill ski? What's wrong with weighting the *uphill ski*?

If you want to climb a ladder you put it against the wall at a certain angle to be safe. If the base is too far away from the wall then it will slide away. This will result in a nasty accident should you be twenty feet up with a glue pot pasting up the Wonderbra ad.

Apply the ladder analogy to your weight on skis (forget the Wonderbra ad for a moment – if you are able to).

For example, you are about to perform a text book christie stop on a steep hill upsides from your friends, who are ogling your dashing performance. With mounting panic you realise that there is not enough room to stop without taking them all out, so you adopt the famous flying-parallel-daisy-chopper. Almost parallel to the hill you try to execute this emergency braking procedure. You go way beyond the critical angle of lean, and you do a spectacular wipe out. Your friends are mightily impressed as long as you haven't knocked them all for six.

This is the extreme, the critical moment when, with a combination of speed and the weight pushing it, the ski cannot recover.

SECRETS OF BETTER SKIING

There are slight differences between the ladder slipping and the ski slipping as the ladder is stationary before it starts moving and there are other considerations such as slope angles, surface conditions, and angulation, but the main similarity is where the **centre of weight** is in relation to each ski.

Imagine a skier standing still on an average slope. The further the centre of weight is away from the downhill ski (ie: uphill), the closer it will be to an uncontrollable slip sliding away. Now if we bring the centre of weight directly over the ski it should not in theory slide sideways at all (as long as the slope is not too steep). It will just hold its position through **static friction**. The more we move the centre of weight away uphill from a vertical position over the ski, the more chance there is of a side slip. You have probably seen this countless times when a skier comes to a bit of mountain unexpectedly steep, leans into the mountain, and the skis slide away from him.

Therefore we put the weight mostly over the downhill ski to maximise the lateral stability of the *ski* on the snow, but we don't put all of it on the lower ski because we want to maximise the *body's* lateral stability by letting our centre of weight swing between the two skis (as long as our legs are slightly apart). In short we do it to maintain balance - a little weight on the top ski but most of it on the lower ski.

So why don't we put most of the weight on the top ski and a little on the lower ski? After all we'd still have the centre of weight between the two skis and there would still be a ski with most of the weight over it giving good static friction. Not only that, our weight would *always* be more over the uphill ski than the lower as the uphill leg on the inside of the turn would have less of a tendency than the lower outside leg to slide away.

It is true that our weight *would* be more over the ski but remember that if we put our weight on the uphill ski, then it is the *uphill* edge of the uphill ski that we are balancing on. This means that we have very little manoeuvre with our lateral balance if we want to *keep* most of our weight on the uphill ski.

Our balance would have to be near perfect as we run along on a knife edge. We don't have a spare leg upsides of our uphill ski to support us. Geddit? I have noticed snowboarders sometimes running their uphill arms along the snow for balance because they only have one edge after all, but it is impractical for us real skiers.

Having said all this there *is* a strong case for skiing as much as possible on the uphill ski but our balance must be good. There are several occasions in this book that I write about transferring weight to the uphill ski during a turn. The transfer takes place after the skier has crossed the fall line (otherwise it would not be the uphill ski!) in the form of a step up, and is known as lateral projection. Racers do it all the time as an integral part of certain turns or when they need to gain height. Experienced skiers will do it on long fast turns for fun to gain speed on a fast traverse as all the movement is forwards; there is virtually no chance of a braking side slip as there could be on the lower ski. Added to this (which I mention elsewhere), it makes for better control transferring from one edge to another on the *same* ski, rather than from one ski to the other.

There are also occasions when we suddenly find ourselves on the uphill ski when we didn't intend to. Far from being a traumatic experience we should relish the moment and it will pass all too quickly. Be comfortable with spending the odd unexpected moment on the uphill ski and you find that it will sometimes get you out of a lot of trouble.

What you will find strange is the sudden precision of the steering on an uphill edge, and to begin with it may throw you off. There is a much more attractive margin for error with lateral weight shift and slide slipping or edging on the downhill ski than on the uphill ski where you will need to be far more precise with your weight placement.

SIMON DEWHURST

11 – SNOW TYPES & HOW TO SKI THEM

One of the best moments on a ski holiday has got to be drawing back the curtains on the first morning, opening the window, and breathing in the fresh mountain air. The view is spectacular, the early morning sun is just touching the tip of the Matterhorn, and you can feel the hairs up your nose freezing.

As you sit down and tuck in to an enormous Swiss breakfast you are already computing the weather and snow conditions aren't you? The fact that the sun is shining in a clear blue sky bodes well, but what about the hairs freezing up your nose? This means that the snow is going to have that squeaky sound when you walk on it, and if you go high up first thing the snow crystals could even be hard and sharp enough to stop your skis running at all.

The effect that different types of snow have on your skiing is quite important. If you did go high up the mountain, it could be really frustrating if you found your skis wouldn't slide! In this instance you would have to wax them first, or else wait for the sun to warm up the snow, or perhaps stay lower down the mountain. If it is this cold your nose and any other exposed parts would be suffering anyway as the air temperature would be minus 10 Celsius or below.

The following snow types cover most of what you are likely to come across. There are more than likely some I have missed out because I have never come across them myself; I would be most grateful for any additions.

RED SNOW AT ANY TEMPERATURE

This is interesting stuff and as far as I know is restricted to Western Europe. The red stuff comes from the Sahara Desert and is the result of a sand storm lifted high into the atmosphere by tropical maritime air which then dumps it on the Alps. It is usually more pink than red and has no bearing on performance whatsoever.

ICE

Ice usually refers to frozen snow that lies on the downside of bumps, slopes that have caught the sun during the day and refrozen over night, or occasionally, after a period of thaw, when everything freezes. This last example is also known as boiler plate and is a killer on the ankles and any other parts that come into contact with it. Very occasionally you may find blue ice from a frozen stream or another water source that has been running across the slope and then frozen overnight. This is best avoided although you can ski over small patches holding your breath and trusting your balance.

To ski on smooth ice successfully, and by smooth ice I mean the first two examples, you must have sharp edges and use them as much as possible. Angulation and hard work are the only successful remedies. If you are skiing hard on icy slopes your skis should be sharpened every day! Many years ago while I was learning to ski slalom gates in Norway we once had a three week period with no new snow at all. At the start of the three weeks the temperature had gone above freezing and turned the slope into an up ended ice rink. We were sharpening our skis twice a day on this stuff! It did have its advantages though. Ten people would come down the same course and make little imprint on the track, so we only had to make new courses twice a day. The main problem was getting the slalom poles, which were trimmed birch saplings and quite solid, into the ice and we had to use a giant wrecking bar. It kept us fit, but there was not a lot of edge or sole left on the bottom of our skis after three weeks!

Ski Maintenance for Ice

Unless you are very rich or have a very good friend in the ski shop you are gong to have to sharpen your own skis. As this is the only maintenance I was going to talk about, I may as well go into it here as it does not really warrant a whole chapter of its own.

This is a bit like a cooking recipe. You will need a *new* file, as they wear out quite quickly. A ten inch bastard mill is the best, but any standard milled file is adequate. You will need a carborundum block - that's a sharpening stone. Make sure you have some oil to go with it although I have used spit quite successfully. You will need one of those decorator's scrapers made of stainless steel. They are about six inches by three and have sharp edges. If they get blunt from use then you can sharpen them on the file. You will also need a rag to wipe any mess off the bottom of the skis. All this stuff can be bought in a hardware store for about $10.

This will probably save you about $100 you would have spent in the ski shop on the same bits. I hope you appreciate the money I am saving you.

If you haven't got a vice readily available – do you mean to say you forgot to pack that huge lump of metal bolted to your workbench in the garage? In that case you can quite easily do all this by hand. First of all get the ski stoppers out of the way with a looped piece of string over the top of each ski or any other way that keeps them held back. It is better to sharpen the edges before scraping the soles as you may get some of the filings sticking to the soles if you do it the other way round. Take a ski and put it on its edge with the back end on the floor. You should stand astride it holding it up with your thighs - not *that* high. Hold the ski with whichever hand you're not going to file the edge with. The ski is roughly at 45 degrees to the floor. File the edge from the shovel end with the file as flat as possible but held at an angle of about 45 degrees *across* the edge. This maximises the cutting of the file. As you work down the ski try to keep one motion going. You will have to walk down the ski as you go, and if you have to stop filing, hold the file at that spot, rearrange yourself, and carry on. You can either kneel down as you work towards the back end, or else drop the shovel onto the ground and put the heel up against the wall to finish off.

There are three more edges to do like this - if you are in a hurry you can just do the two inside edges of each ski as long as you remember to put them on right. Mark the skis left and right if you are doing this. If the file is doing its job you should land up with a load of metal filings along your filing fingers, and you should only need to run it along each edge a couple of times at the most. You will only need to do it more if there are really bad gouges in the metal. You may only have to run the file along once; I'll let you be the judge.

You should now do the bottom. Put the ski upside down at 45 degrees against a wall with the tip on the wall and the heel on the floor. You can again steady the ski between your thighs. Get the file at its maximum cutting angle of 45 degrees across the sole and draw it back down the ski with quite a bit of pressure. Again you should feel some bits of metal on your fingers. Remember not to go over the same bits but stop the file if you want to rearrange things.

Oil the carborundum up and do the same on the edges and the sole that you have done with the file. This can be done quite lightly and is only intended to smooth off the burrs made by the file's rougher treatment. Remember to keep it as flat as possible. You can now just blunt off the first six inches at the tips *very* lightly with the carborundum held at 45 degrees across the edges. This means that the skis won't cut into the ice too quickly at the beginning of a turn. I've never noticed if this works but the purist theoretician in me says it does, so there we go.

Scraping the sole comes next. Take the decorator's scraper between forefinger and thumb of both hands and draw it up the sole of the ski at about 45 degrees. Everything on this job seems to be done at 45 degrees so for a change let's say 35 degrees. You will be using the long side of the scraper to do this of course. The scraper's sharp edge should shave off small amounts of the plastic sole. If you bend the scraper up in the middle fractionally then you will get a minimal concave sole which can theoretically mean a faster edge set, but again I can't say I've ever noticed the difference between doing it and not doing it. Scraping the sole is really only done to clear up the mess made by the file and to equalise the amount of edge taken off by the file.

Finally wipe the skis with that valuable rag to get off any loose bits of metal, oil, and plastic.

It goes without saying but I'll say it anyway. If you want to avoid all this hassle leave your skis in the ski shop overnight and ask the technician to do it for you. It may cost a few bucks but will give you more time to read *Secrets of Better Skiing*.

SNOW WITH AIR TEMPERATURE ABOVE 0°C

Fresh snow

Melting snow affects the running of the skis in two ways. The first time that it melts it slows the skis down. Freshly fallen overnight snow late in the season has this effect as the air temperature rises above freezing in the morning. Rain does the same job as it falls on to fresh snow. If you can imagine skiing through strawberry jam then you will know the stuff I'm talking about. Off piste can be hell in this awful stuff if the air temperature is above freezing. As it has not been packed the skis go into it a few inches. It is very bad for the knee ligaments and the ego, and should be avoided. If this crud has been flattened it also tends to hold water, which makes it even less attractive. In these sort of conditions and if it's raining as well, you'd be better off going round an art gallery for the day.

Old snow (sometimes Spring snow)

Once this snow has thawed and refrozen for a few days and nights, however, it takes on the consistency of sugar when it starts to thaw again. This type of snow presents the least friction of any type to a ski, and as long as only the top few centimetres are melting, it provides an excellent surface to ski on as I have mentioned before. One memorable run down through the woods in Verbier Switzerland was on this sugar snow. It was early spring and the birds were singing, and we were skiing in bright sunshine and *rain showers*! We were hot anyway and in shirtsleeves, so the rain had a pleasant cooling effect.

With old sugar snow the melt water drops down through the existing snow and runs away, so no water *appears* to lie on the surface. I say 'appears' in italics because only the top layer is actually melting and so there *is* water, but only from around the crystals on the surface.

Note also that snow melts near rocks quicker than on open ground. The rock conducts heat from all its surfaces and snow three or four feet down for maybe six inches all round the rock will melt. This causes a pleasant little trap for the unwary as they can ski up to a warm looking, moss covered rock for a sit down, take their skis off, and schlunk - they drop some way into a nice warm hole.

Remember that snow insulates itself and reflects heat so until the air temperature gets quite high it is only the top layer that melts. As the temperature rises the snow begins to melt further down. At this stage off piste skiing becomes impractical and even dangerous. Solid bridges over crevasses will start to weaken and glaciers become off limits. Added to this there is a higher risk of avalanches later in the day.

Remember that *all* snow is at freezing point or lower.

SNOW FROM 0°C TO -10°C DEGREES

This is the stuff that you see on holiday brochures. On the piste and compacted by a machine and countless ski tracks, it provides a reliable and consistent surface with low friction and just enough give to help braking manoeuvres. You know the sort of stuff I mean.

Off piste and untouched with a little hut in the background and all white and sparkly, it will vary in consistency depending on wind and position. As you stand by the lodge window at night mesmerised by the snowflakes falling past the window all you can think about is the metre of powder tomorrow. The cold air tripping along behind such a dump will usually guarantee good conditions, although that amount of snow does need some time to stabilise before it is safe. As I mention in the chapter on avalanches the crystals need to settle into each other so that the snow condenses and it becomes one huge interconnected carpet of angel poop.

If you look out of the window and the snow is coming down almost horizontally that means the wind is blowing, or you're lying on the floor after too much gluwein; this puts a slightly different slant on things out there on the mountainside. I'm referring to the wind not the gluwein.

On any windward slope the snow crystals will be compressed by the wind into a solid crust, whose thickness will depend on the length of the storm and the amount of the snowfall, and quite possibly the temperature at which they fell. If there is already some nice powder snow that fell before the storm, there may only be a thin crust, which you will probably break through. It is still heavy duty survival skiing. Some people can power through it like an arctic ice breaker applying normal deep snow technique, but I usually have to make quite violent jump turns until I can find a way out of it. A nice caramelised creme brulee in a good restaurant is infinitely preferable.

The worst kind of this rubbish is the crust that feels like skiing on a hard piste and bears your weight for a while then all of a sudden gives way. You fall through the hole, stop dead, and are catapulted out of your skis. They nose dive into the deep snow below, and you spend the rest of a nice sunny morning looking for them.

A solid weight bearing crust is skiable but the rills formed by the wind do not make it that brilliant. If the crust is four or five inches thick then you can always make an igloo. All you need to do is cut blocks about 18 inches by 9 with your skis (don't forget to take your tape measure with you) and jam the blocks together in a spiral, not forgetting to slant them in as you go.....

On any leeward slope out of the wind there could be some excellent powder skiing, not only from fallen snow but also from spin drift blown from the windward slopes. The tell tale sign of good hidden powder like this is the cornice formed at the watershed – or should it be 'snowshed' – between a windy and sheltered slope.

I have a feeling that if anyone from Utah or the nether regions of the Canadian Rockies is reading this, they will be a little bemused by the efforts us Europeans make to find good powder. Well the truth is that after a few days off piste in the Alps gets a bit crowded and can become skied out pretty quickly. We also don't get as much snow as you guys.

SNOW LOWER THAN -10°C DEGREES

If you are skiing when the temperature is this low then you are going to know about it. All exposed parts are going to feel really cold at speed and there is the danger of localised frostbite. The snow crystals are sharp enough to slow the skis down (which may or may not be a good idea!), and you will have to wax the bottom of the skis to get them to run properly.

If the air temperature is lower than -20 then you will have to be careful with your breathing as unthawed ice and snow crystals could give you a sore throat.

GLOSSARY

Angel poop The lightest deepest powder snow.

Angulation The bending of the knees, usually into the slope, to set an edge. The hips also have to be bent in order to keep the weight in the desired position. With little or no edge set the knees will be bent directly over the skis. With maximum edge set they will bend in towards the slope.

Anticipation Preparation made before a turn with the hands, eyes, soles of the feet, and **longitudinal** weight shift. When learning new technique it can also mean a **pole plant**, and is more often than not accompanied by **angulation.**

Avalanche Something that will kill you unless you are careful. With the introduction to shorter skis allowing easier off-piste skiing, and the forecast for heavier snowfalls as the world warms up, the danger of avalanches cannot be over stressed. Anyone who skis off-piste should only do so if they know about the avalanche risks at any given time in the area they are skiing in, or is going with someone who does. A public notice stating that the overall avalanche risk in the resort is low, does not mean that a *particular* area is safe and checks should always be made if in doubt.

Avalament From the French 'avaler', to swallow. Take it to mean an absorption of a bump by lifting the legs ie: there is angulation but it comes from *lifting the legs* rather than *lowering the body*.

Balance The ability to keep the weight in the desired position. Balance is acquired by mileage and is more readily acquired by very small children. It can also be helped by being fit, having good eyesight, and learning to feel snow conditions through the soles of the feet. **Longitudinal balance** refers to movement of the centre of weight between the front and back of both skis, while **latitudinal balance** refers to weight variations between and across the skis.

Body Position The direction a skier is facing at any given moment in relation to his skis, and refers to his upper body above the hips.

Boiler plate The most appalling stuff to ski on. Churned up melted snow that has refrozen. Avoid at all costs - ankle snapping rubbish.

Camber The upward arc, rather like a bow, built into a ski from the **shovel** to the **tail** to provide tension when the ski is weighted.

Carving The arc made by a ski on its edge when the ski is under enough tension to produce *substantial* **reverse camber**. Because the ski has been bent so much, carving produces an arc of *smaller* radius than merely **edging**.

Centre of Gravity (or Centre of Mass) Theoretically speaking this is the point on a skier where an imaginary plane running through the skier in any direction would bisect a skier's weight equally. For example, if we were to skewer him at this point without his skis and boots on, he would revolve evenly on a spit, being perfectly balanced and thus perfectly cooked right through.

Centre of Weight The same as the **centre of gravity** but for our purposes we take it to mean the point on the ground vertically below the **centre of gravity** (onto a horizontal plane) where a skier's weight is centered at any given time. If the centre of weight is more than a critical distance from the middle of the skis and the feet at any given time, he will usually lose his balance. Various forces will alter this radius of latitude ie: gravity, forward and sideways movement, the steepness of the slope and the type of snow. By deduction, lowering the **centre of gravity** will give a skier more chance to stay within the radius of latitude. This raises an interesting question - why do small children learn to ski so much quicker than big adults?

Chord length The distance between the two bits of the ski touching the ground (the **shovel** and the **tail**) when the ski is lying on a flat surface. This is the distance usually used to denote a ski's length. They used to be made in 5cm increments but now skis come in all sizes.

Christie Another name for a parallel turn reputedly invented in Christiania, Norway during the nineteenth century.

Contre Virage French for 'against the turn'. An extra bit of turn tacked on to the end of a main turn. As a skier comes to the end of a turn he can either drop quickly down a fraction thereby **unweighting** the skis, or else contra rotate thereby **steering** the skis. The tails can then move round enabling him to initiate an edge set.

Contre Rotation French for contra rotation ... a twisting of the **upper body** into the slope (sometimes initiated by a small movement across the body with the lower hand) to enable the tails of the skis to slide round (see above).

Corn Spring snow and the most flattering stuff to ski on.

Cornice The overhang of snow with attendant cliff formed on crests and ridges by windy conditions. Looks rather like a frozen wave.

Couloir Also known as a corrie, avalanche chute, and a gully, this is a steep narrow passage between rocks. Couloirs should always be approached and skied with care.

Crud Glutinous new snow that has been rained on and not had a chance to re freeze. Best avoided.

Dynamic friction The friction between the snow and a moving ski. It is less than **static friction**.

Edge Set See **Setting an edge**.

Edging Putting the skis on their edge by angulating. The radius of the arc formed by just an edged ski is greater than a carved ski as there is no substantial **reverse camber** involved.

ELP Short for English lavatory position (or ALP for American/Australian LP). This is a natural position sometimes adopted at the early stages of learning and recommended at any time when good balance is in doubt, and is not just a mild joke. By bending both the hips and knees over the middle of the skis with the legs several inches apart the centre of gravity is lowered and the centre of weight has more room for **latitudinal** and **longitudinal** movement.

SECRETS OF BETTER SKIING

Eyes Using them correctly is the most important part of the **anticipation** process. Looking slightly further ahead than you would on your feet can help a lot.

Fall Line An imaginary line describing the steepest route down a mountain. The fall line may change direction owing to bumps and dips. Imagine the route a marble would take down a slope without jumping.

Falling A very important part of the learning process.

Feet After your eyes your feet are the most sensitive and most important parts of your body when it comes to skiing. Look after them as well as a wood louse would look after his antennae.

Fitness Just as important as learning to fall.

Freestyle Doing everything on skis that involves more than skiing down a piste doing the odd turn. It includes moguls, jumps, half pipes, skiing through people's front doors, along their kitchen units, and out through their patio windows and over a balcony etc etc.

Jet Turn Not used much for recreational skiing nowadays, this involves a quick avalment accompanied by a backwards and sideways (downhill) weight shift.

Lateral Projection Transferring weight from the downhill to the uphill ski while moving on a traverse.

Latitudinal See **Balance**.

Longitudinal See **Balance**.

Natural Torsion The ability of the thigh and abdominal muscles and ligaments to act like a twisted rubber band.

Piste Prepared route down a mountainside. Known as a trail in North America.

Pole Plant A crucial part of **anticipation** during the process of learning new techniques.

Poles Crucial accessories for a pole plant. In fact it is impossible to do a pole plant without them. They should be 5cm (2 inches) shorter than you have been used to.

Reverse Camber The arc formed in a ski by applying pressure down on it from above. The more reverse camber is applied to a ski, the shorter becomes the radius of the arc. Short radius turns are made for short turns and long radius turns for long turns. See **carving**

Royal Christie A flat turn on one ski while the other ski is lifted high in the air behind the skier.

Self Assessment Deciding which of the five grades of skier you fit into.

Setting an Edge Unweighting a ski by a sudden down movement at the end of a turn. The weight on the ski then increases and brakes it against the snow in preparation for the next turn. An **edge set** is used in short turns. The angle of an edge set in relation to the **fall line** will vary according to the degree a skier wants to brake eg: on a very steep slope the angle would be 90 degrees to the fall line, and on a blue run perhaps only 30 degrees.

Shovel The front bit of a ski just behind the tip that is touching the snow. Also useful for digging your car out of the snow.

Sidecut The arcs formed on each side of the ski (when looked at from above) to allow the potential for **reverse camber**.

Skis Things you ski on.

Snowplough/Wedge/Stem The V shaped beginners turn - and hang on to for too long if not taught something more useful quite soon.

Static Friction The amount of friction between two objects that are in contact but are stationary. We are talking skis on snow here. There is much more friction between ski and snow when the skis are stationary than when they are moving. The friction between a moving ski and the snow is known as **dynamic friction**.

Steering Turning a ski by *applying* weight

Stem Christie A turn that starts with a snowplough, wedge or stem and finishes with a christie or parallel turn.

Step up Taking a definitive step up while moving on a traverse from the inside edge of the downhill ski to the outside edge of the uphill ski. It is very similar to **lateral projection** and if you are a gardener about as difficult to tell apart as oregano and marjoram.

Style Something of little interest to the better skier

Tail The back of a ski.

The Tuck The classic aerodynamic position adopted by racers to gain maximum speed, and by beginners going at ten miles an hour who feel like downhill racers. (It's strange that racers always appear to be grimacing in the tuck, while beginners are always smiling!) From an up right position to the tuck the acceleration on a medium to steep slope can be considerable, and should therefore be used with care.

Thief Someone who steals your skis. Always separate them outside a restaurant. If you can't find them later, wait till everyone's gone home. There should be two left. If there's only one ski home carefully, and be on the look-out for a one legged thief. Before accusing someone, don't forget to ask yourself how many skis you had on when arriving at the restaurant.

Torque The twisting movement of a ski. The amount it will twist along its length will affect its performance. Generally, the stiffer the torque, the higher will be the ski's performance.

Trail Prepared route down a mountainside or a path through wooded country. Known as piste in Europe.

Unweighting Turning a ski by taking weight *off* it. An unweighting movement is generally executed by pivoting the tails of the skis around the tips although occasionally a ski can be pivoted around the centre (as in the Wedel turn or learning in the bumps).

Upper body The torso including the arms and head.

Weight The application of weight on to a ski is gauged by the pressure applied by the soles of the feet. As a general rule weight is kept on the middle of the foot, and seldom moves more than an inch or two either backwards or forwards (longitudinal) to get the desired result. The distribution of weight between the two skis (latitudinal) can vary from all on one ski to an equal spread between the two.

Wipe Out A great sixties record from Cliff Richard's band, the Shadows. Also a crash of stupendous proportions which gets better with the telling.

SIMON DEWHURST

RULES OF THE SLOPES

The International Ski Federation (FIS) has published ten very important rules, which are internationally recognised, in order to ensure safety while skiing.

1 **Respect for others** – a skier must behave in such a way that he does not endanger or prejudice others.

2 **Control of Speed Skiing** – a skier must be in control. He must adopt his speed and manner of skiing to his personal ability and to the prevailing conditions of terrain, snow and weather, as well as to the density of traffic.

3 **Choice of Route** – a skier coming from behind must choose his route in such a way that he does not endanger skiers ahead. **The skier or snowboarder in front has priority.**

4 **Overtaking** – a skier may overtake another skier above or below and to the right or to the left, provided that he leaves enough space for the overtaken skier to make any voluntary or involuntary movement.

5 **Entering and Starting** – a skier entering a marked run or starting again after stopping must look up and down the piste or trail in narrow places or where the visibility is restricted. After a fall in such a place, a skier must move clear of the piste or trail as soon as possible.

6 **Stopping on the Piste or Trail** – unless absolutely necessary, a skier must avoid stopping on the piste or trail in narrow places, or where visibility is restricted.

7 **Climbing and Descending on Foot** – skiers climbing and descending on foot must keep to the side of the piste or trail.

8 **Respect for Signs and Markings** – a skier must obey all signs and markings - they are there for your safety.

9 **Assistance** – in case of accidents, provide help and alert the rescue service.

10 **Identification** – every skier and witness, whether a responsible party or not, must exchange names and addresses following an accident.

All **the above rules are binding by law** and apply to both skiers and snowboarders alike. You should also be aware that the penalties for breaking the laws in different countries can vary considerably – lift pass confiscation to imprisonment and a heavy fine to name the extremes.

SIMON DEWHURST

OFF PISTE AND OFF TRAIL RULES

Be aware that in certain countries some of the rules below are also enforceable by law, and that in the event of a accident the costs for rescuing an injured skier can be considerable.

1 If you don't know the area, **book a local guide.**

2 **Check weather reports** with the local tourist office or local piste or trail security officials before going off-piste to ensure the area you are going to is safe.

3 **Don't ski off-piste on your own.**

4 **Don't assume you are safe by following tracks or skiers** in front of you, as they may not know the area either.

5 When skiing off-piste be aware of the risks of skiing in an unmarked, unpatrolled area and **make sure you let someone know where you are going**. (Arrange a rendezvous afterwards to let them know you are back safely.)

6 **Your insurance policy must cover you** for off-piste skiing.

7 Consider hiring or buying a **good up-to-date avalanche bleeper**

If in doubt about the conditions or your ability NEVER leave marked runs.

Printed in Great Britain
by Amazon